SPORTS
DRIVING

SPORTS DRIVING

A Complete Guide to Horse Driving Trials

AMANDA SAVILLE

Phographs are by Liza Pern with additional photography by Elspeth Houston and Bennington Carriages. The line drawings on pages 139 and 142 are by Ann Hughes.

Copyright © 2007 Amanda Saville

First published in the UK in 2007
by Kenilworth Press, an imprint of Quiller Publishing Ltd

British Library Cataloguing-in-Publication Data
 A catalogue record for this book
 is available from the British Library

ISBN 978 1 905693 01 6

Printed in China

Kenilworth Press
An imprint of Quiller Publishing Ltd
Wykey House, Wykey, Shrewsbury, SY4 1JA
Tel: 01939 261616 Fax: 01939 261606
E-mail: info@quillerbooks.com
Website: www.kenilworthpress.com

Contents

HRH The Duke of Edinburgh competing with HM The Queen's team of Fell ponies.

I would imagine that people have been driving horses for almost as long as they have been riding them. For thousands of years, horse-drawn transport was the principal way of moving about. Then the internal combustion engine came along, and horses were no longer required for purely practical purposes.

However, horses continued to be ridden for various sports, and in 1970 the International Equestrian Federation published the first international rules for carriage driving competitions. These were based on the existing rules for ridden 3 Day Events. These rules are the basis of sports driving, and the subject of this book.

A great deal has happened since 1970. Many more people have taken to driving carriages in competitions. Furthermore, experience and new materials have been responsible for the introduction of a whole range of innovations to the design of carriages and materials for harness. These have made the sport less hazardous, and greatly improved the lot of the horses and ponies.

This book contains practically everything a beginner needs to know about the sport, and, in particular - as they are required to do all the work - about the training and care of the horses and ponies.

Author's Note

Throughout the book I use both metric and imperial measurements as the horse world still mixes these along with 'hands' for measuring horses (one hand is four inches).

Acknowledgements

I am very honoured that HRH The Duke of Edinburgh has written the Foreword to this book and I am most grateful for his constructive comments and suggestions on the manuscript. Any omissions or errors are however of course entirely my responsibility.

It is hard to find the words to thank Liza Pern for her incredible support, patience and endless encouragement. Her practical ability keeps a hold on my enthusiasm and channels it in the right direction. This book would never have happened without her (sorry about the extra grey hairs!). Thanks also to my husband John, who copes with ponies day in and day out and still smiles!

I would also like to thank Gay for her support over many years, which has enabled me to follow my dream of carriage driving. Thanks also go to my fantastic team who keep the 'home fires burning' when we are on the road and those who travel around the country with us.

'The latest 4 x 4!'

Introduction

There are several disciplines under the carriage driving umbrella. Sports Driving is the focus of this book, but along with Private Driving, Coaching, Scurry and Pleasure Driving, it is just one of the ways to enjoy the thrill and exhilaration of horses. Each discipline has its own traditions and skills; we will clarify those of Sports Driving and, hopefully, bridge some of the divides that cause confusion between traditional and modern driving. To put the sport in context, let's just take a very quick look at the history of carriage driving.

Wheeled vehicles have been around for thousands of years pulled by a variety of animals depending on the country and the need. Competitive driving can be traced right back to the Greeks and Romans. Pottery evidence of chariot races exists from the Mycenaean people around 1500BC and in Homer's *Iliad* he describes a chariot race at a wealthy nobleman's funeral. The race consisted of one lap around a tree stump and the winner received a female slave as his prize! By tradition, the Olympic Games was founded on chariot racing around 680BC by the Greeks. There were four horse and two horse races with jockeys chosen for their lightness (so they were often only teenagers). The races began as a procession into a 'hippodrome' followed by twelve laps of the course with sharp and dangerous turns round posts at each end watched by as many as ten thousand spectators. These races were often violent and deadly, using modified wooden war chariots with open backs.

Chariots: ancient and modern. The author with her version which actually show jumps as well!

Roman chariot racing was influenced by the Greeks and the Etruscans. In ancient Rome the main venue was the Circus Maximus which could seat 250,000 people. Races consisted of seven laps around the track, the chariots being 'sprung' together at the start from mechanical gates. Racers were considered professionals and there was widespread betting – many races were held daily, over much of the year. Their charioteers were often slaves but, if successful, could win both money and their freedom. The horses also could become famous and the Romans kept detailed records of pedigrees, breeds and individual names of winners. The infamous Emperor Nero was a fanatical charioteer, winning at the Olympic Games. He further developed racing into a format which used four specific teams identified by colour who would compete against each other. These teams took on characteristics of their own as the sport grew, collaborating with each other against other teams. Individual charioteers could be traded between teams for a fee, much as footballers are today.

In Britain an early mention of the chariot is of Queen Boadicea riding at the head of her Iceni hordes to challenge the Roman invaders. During the Middle Ages throughout Europe most travellers, who could afford to, would ride in a carriage though, as they had no springs at that stage, it can't have been particularly comfortable! Closed carriages began to be more widely used by the upper classes in the sixteenth century. Better sprung vehicles were developed during the seventeenth century, followed by lighter and more fashionable ones from the mid-eighteenth century. Coachbuilders and artisans of various skills worked together to produce, not just state coaches for weddings and funerals, but vehicles that were comfortable, speedy and smart for pleasure and parades.

It all changed in the mid-1800s when the railways became the faster modern alternative to the coach followed closely by the automobile in the 1890s. No longer the primary mode of travel, 'coaching' became an upper-class gentleman's sport in Britain and America. The first driving 'clubs' were effectively diners' clubs whose members met together on a regular basis in London and drove to the country to dine. The first of these was the Richmond Driving Club started in 1838, although these clubs were shortlived due to the Crimean War. After this war the Four-in-Hand Club was founded with the Duke of Beaufort as its patron and a limited membership of thirty. However, four-in-hand driving became more and more popular and the Coaching Club was formed in 1871. It still exists to this day with members meeting at least once a year to drive and dine.

The two World Wars and the advent of the car meant there was little finance or enthusiasm for carriage driving in Britain in the first half of the twentieth century. The Queen's coronation in 1953 when

the Coaching Club brought in sufficient carriages to transport all the Commonwealth prime ministers encouraged new interest in driving. The British Driving Society was founded in 1957 with Area Commissioners around the country whose brief was to organise driving meets, picnics and other social or instructional events. Horse shows began to introduce driving classes with black and yellow rosettes being awarded to BDS members who competed. In 1958 The Royal Windsor Horse Show hosted the BDS's inaugural event. Windsor went on to become one of the most popular and famous venues, where members had the opportunity to drive around the Castle and Home Park. This remains an extremely well attended annual event.

In 1969 Prince Philip who was then the President of the FEI (Fédération Equestre Internationale) – the governing body of equestrian sports – first witnessed four-in-hand turnouts competing in Germany where competitions were already well established. With the help of Colonel Mike Ansell, then Chairman of the FEI Committee, and other European experts, the first international

An early tandem in Horse Driving Trials with hula hoops on the back wheels to make the width for cones in the days before extending axles.

carriage driving rules were drawn up. These were based loosely on the ridden three-day event format to include dressage, obstacles and cones. Although these rules have since undergone (and continually undergo) regular review, the format still remains fundamentally the same. Carriage Driving became an FEI discipline in 1970.

The British Horse Driving Trials Association was set up in 1996 to oversee and organise competitive events in the UK. Club and National events are held regularly throughout the year. World Championships take place every other year, including Single Horse Championships, Horse Pairs Championships and Four-in-Hand Championships, as well as competitions at the World Equestrian Games, held every four years. For pony drivers, the World Combined Pony Championships are held every two years and include singles, pairs and four-in-hand.

That is where Sports Driving is at now – but let's wind the clock back two and a half thousand years or so, to the origins of the Olympic Games. With the exception of sailing, the equestrian Olympic disciplines are the only ones in which men and women compete against each other. They are also the only ones in which humans and animals compete together as a team. There are three equestrian disciplines – show jumping, dressage and eventing. Whatever happened to the chariot racing which in the modern day we would call carriage driving? It is no longer considered worthy of being an Olympic sport. On a personal note I feel this is incredibly sad – it is just as skilled as eventing, using the same features of dressage, obstacles (cross-country equivalent) and cones (show jumping equivalent). Horses have to be at the top of their fitness, with all the training and flexibility required of a ridden equestrian discipline. Drivers have to be at the top of their game with regard to skills, knowledge and physical ability. We have European and World Championships in the sport – why is it excluded from the Olympics?

Oh well – that is not what this book is about. Whether you want to get started from scratch and just enjoy the countryside, or 'get the bug' and explore the competitive (and social!) aspects of sports driving – the guidance is similar. The fundamentals are: understanding your pony, your equipment and knowing how to operate in safety. For those of you already involved in driving we will cover all aspects of training, including the much 'feared' discipline of dressage as well as the speedier bits! Whoever you are, we are both united in the passion of driving and horses. Welcome to a wonderful way of life!

Entering the 'driving world' can be quite a daunting thought but, as soon as you talk to a 'driver', doors will open. They are a fabulous bunch of people, longing to share their enthusiasm for their sport. You may have a chum who drives, have seen a display or competition, or have an outgrown pony chomping its way through

your pension fund! I think the first practical step is to get onto the back of a carriage to feel the thrill, without having the responsibility of control and direction. There are numerous Clubs affiliated to the British Horse Driving Trials Association as well as a dedicated group of Sports Drivers providing opportunities to 'try driving'. Contacting these organisations will point you in the right direction for your area, details of many of them are in the reference section at the back of this book. This will lead you to a group of people who in the beginning had the same questions and anxieties that you may now be feeling. These will pale into insignificance as soon as the passion takes over. Offering to help at a Club event will provide you with experience and knowledge before you arrive with your own turnout, not to mention making you extremely popular with event organisers! It will also expose you to many different types of equipment and horses/ponies, thus helping you to decide what you will be comfortable with.

I would advocate finding an enthusiastic mentor who can channel you in the right direction and answer many of your questions. A number of drivers whom I have helped into driving have had the preconceived idea that 'Oooh, I'm a bit old'. Equally, parents often feel that their child may be too young. Utter nonsense! As long as you understand English and can breathe – we can bring you the sheer joy of driving!

Often when I am talking to riders they express horror at the thought of carriage driving as they feel 'the pony is so far away from me'. True, but the skill of driving is in the use of your hands and voice to communicate. This in turn brings you closer to your pony as you have to develop a strong bond of trust between you both. Some children I have taught to ride have not always been comfortable 'on top', but due to their love of ponies, have wanted to persevere and

Above Left:
The Galloping Granny! Meg came to driving late after her family had grown up, thanks to a birthday gift of a driving lesson. She's never looked back and has achieved superb results in competition.

Above Right:
Meg's granddaughter Katy, winning a junior club competition at four years old.

A happy team result! The Scottish Raiders at the Indoor Finals in 2005. Two National titles and eight placings.

have taken to driving like ducks to water. Some have even gone on to win at National Junior Competition level. The same applies to adults who feel they want the freedom of riding but find lack of natural balance, disability or prior injury an issue. Their fear of falling off curtails any relaxation or enjoyment they would otherwise experience. I have had so much fun getting these people going in a carriage; the feedback of their laughter and enjoyment is quite wonderful.

We're going places – let's take you.

From little to large – all
suitable driving equines
and their drivers!

2 The Equine

Well we have got as far as deciding that driving is going to be interesting – actually there's little hope for you now! Once on the slippery slope to addiction, it takes over your life, but it needn't take over your bank account. It is as expensive as you want to make it or can afford.

If you haven't had any lessons in driving or been out with a friend, then I strongly advise you to do so early on. As Sports Driving is your interest, then do go to a centre, or to an individual who already participates in the discipline of horse driving trials, so your learning can be suited to what you hope to achieve. Most people who come to me to learn do so with an 'I fancy trying driving but don't know what to expect' comment. After the first session they are saying 'I had no idea it was such fun, I want more of this!' That is probably because we use ponies around 12hh, in a two-wheel carriage and 'double reins', so the instructor can take over at any time, which instils confidence in the client. This leads nicely onto the subject of suitable equines.

Many of you will have a pony who is not really justifying his keep any more, but you love him and wouldn't dream of selling him on. He could be ideal. Ponies are much less intimidating to learn with and start competing. A horse is quite awesome and a team of horses is absolutely stunning but, in reality, is out of reach of most for us. They are also more difficult to deal with if you encounter a hiccup, due to their size and strength. I have enjoyed driving my horses, pair and single, but have pure joy and fun with my ponies. Nothing beats that feeling!

(*Note:* For ease of writing I make reference to 'ponies' and 'him' or 'his'. I am not being sexist or 'height-ist' – just trying to make the reference more uniform and easier to read. So 'pony' in this context means equine of any height.)

If you have a pony that you would like to drive, do be quite objective as to his suitability. Just loving him isn't enough! If he has been ridden, done shows, Pony Club etc, then you are a long way down the line already. Being good in traffic is one of my priorities. It's not funny to get squished into a hedge or spun around in the road with a carriage. Some ponies hate lorries or large vehicles, but with careful thought as to your exercise routes, then you may be able to avoid any such issues, especially if he's perfect in every other way.

If he is nervous with noise behind him, then you will need to take time to get him settled and familiar with this when it comes to breaking him to harness. Do make sure when he is in training that all his flat work is done in an open bridle (no blinkers). It is essential that he can 'see' the noise of the log or tyre and the false shafts on his sides. Then when you are driving with blinkers, and the pony turns to look at you, he doesn't get a surprise.

ABOVE:
Merlion getting a nice lengthened stride, although not enough stretch in his neck in spite of the reins 'giving'.

RIGHT:
Merlion in a ridden schooling session – a little tight in neck and jaw.

Tom Tom, one of our first rescue ponies being logged. Tut tut for not having boots on! Should he have been frightened, then Philip would have stopped him with the lunge line so I didn't have to put undue pressure on his mouth.

Next, think about his size; driving is social, you can have two or three friends or more out with you for a pleasure drive. If you aim to compete with a single, then think about your own size and that of your back-stepper. It is compulsory for two people to be on the carriage at all times in single and pairs competition, and the minimum weight for a single pony carriage is 90kg. So the cute mini-Shetland that is fat, bored and bad tempered will not do for the family outing! However, the standard Shetlands of forty inches are brilliant at club events and I know several who can outpace 14hh ponies – though the walk sections are another matter!

Velvet, a very special Shetland who was occasionally fat but never bored, and gave many larger ponies a run for their money. She won numerous events and helped several youngsters into driving.

Ideally 12hh up to 14hh is a great size to start with. They will cope with most of the questions that will be asked of them, provided their preparation has been correct. So a sensible (and that doesn't mean boring) ridden pony, that has had an all-round education could be driving in three weeks, provided every stage of the harness training is done thoroughly and the pony willingly accepts the questions. Age is no barrier; we have several ponies in their twenties competing with our juniors at Club level.

If you decide to get an untouched youngster, you must be prepared to be patient, as it will take at least eight to ten weeks to get the pony driving and settled into his new career. I know many ponies are broken to driving a lot quicker than this, but they do need time to absorb their new found knowledge. At least four weeks should be devoted to mouthing and long reining. This time spent will be invaluable and set him up for life.

So far we have only looked at the family favourite and the youngster. Before we go any further, is either of them going to suit *your* ambition? The cheapest option may be driving the family riding pony. If you picked up a yearling for £250, add the cost of keep for three years, then add the cost of breaking (maybe up to £1,500) this could still be an option. *But* the pony may not have good paces to suit the dressage phase, or may not be big enough in the long term. He might not have a brave nature, and this is vital if you are to negotiate obstacles at a good speed or he may have some other foible that irritates and these are all considerations. No one breed is

Dark Aura – twenty-nine-year-old stallion still competing regularly with young drivers.

definitely better than another and personal choice usually comes in somewhere along the line of decision making.

If you want to compete regularly and work up to Open classes then choose your native breed carefully, as their paces may not always be appreciated at National level. At Club level however, they can be hard to beat. (I've learned this from personal experience having driven both Shetland and Fell ponies in competition and relied on gaining the advantage in the obstacles and cones!) Welsh ponies, Caspian, Eriskay, Dartmoor Hill ponies, British Spotted, Highland, New Forest – in fact most native breeds are, on the whole, sensible and suitable. Hackney purebreds are often feisty and I would avoid them for first time owners, though when crossed with a native breed they can be very successful. However, there will be indignant howls from devoted fans of several breeds that I may not have mentioned, so I will stop digging before the hole gets too big!

Again with horses, there is no right or wrong breed and most will try to the best of their ability. At the end of the day, temperament rules. If it is suitable, drive it – if not, sell it! I remember a lovely lady, an experienced rider, who had decided to drive a huge horse and both she and her horse were new to the discipline. At her first lesson I asked if she really needed to drive this horse as it was very clear to me that it did not have a suitable attitude. She was adamant, so I never mentioned it again and did as much as I could to create harmony for them. About a year later I had a call to say she was sick of battling with it and had bought a 12.2hh pony and had never been so happy.

Young horse getting 'miles on the clock' showing the groom with a lunge line attached to the head collar for safety. If necessary this can be used to help stop the horse without resorting to huge pressure on the bit.

RIGHT:
Highland pony in a two-wheeler with a backstep: a nice turnout.

BELOW:
The author's pair of rescued Welsh ponies enjoying the obstacles.

If you choose to buy a pony that is already driving, then do make sure you see it being driven, or do so yourself. This sounds so obvious, but many ponies are sold as 'ride and has driven', and this phrase rings alarms bells for me. Very often the pony has had an accident or fright and is not reliable and that is why you must drive it yourself, or take an experienced person with you who can.

When trying your potential pony, make sure you look at him whilst he is being driven because that is the picture the judges are going to see. There are many faults that can be remedied, but if this is your first foray into driving, don't be too sure that you want to sort out any major issues. You need to be driving a safe, fun and interested pony that comes with as few hang-ups as possible at this stage. Once you have a 'few miles' under your belt then use your horsemanship to tackle something more challenging.

On the assumption that you have found what you are looking for, then note the harness, bit and carriage it is going in – is it similar to what you intend to use? For example, is the pony in a four-wheeler – do you only have a two-wheeler? Is the bit a very strong one with a tight curb – why? The whole picture can indicate how the pony goes and his attitude. If you like the look of the pony so far and want to take it further, ask if you can bring your own carriage over to try the pony in it. Sometimes they may not like certain vehicles, or maybe find the feel of a four-wheeler unusual if they are not familiar with one, or vice versa. I once went to buy a horse that had been in a team as a leader and was going beautifully in a two-wheeler. I was impressed and asked to try it in my own four-wheeler – it freaked out completely and it was only thanks to a strong man grabbing hold of us that stopped a certain runaway. The horse obviously hated the carriage and thankfully this was discovered before we got any further down the line with the sale.

There are always dodgy dealers in horses, but there will be more genuine people from whom you can find the right pony, and some very good, reputable internet sites that can help in your search.

Feeding

For a pony working off grass, the fitness required for club events will take longer and is harder to sustain as the constant eating fills the belly and reduces optimum working levels. If you can restrict grazing to just twelve hours and stable for the other twelve hours, this will tighten the muscles and you can then put in a little 'fuel' to help energise the muscles. However, if you are doing pleasure drives and fun days you may not want the pony 'too sharp' for that level. It is the same for a young pony fresh into the sport, and it is better to be a bit 'flat' to begin with while they get used to all the 'ins and outs'.

ABOVE:
Molly and JJ, half brother and sister, very new to pairs driving both going 'flat' but safe ...

ABOVE RIGHT:
... and fat and slow! As they gain experience and fitness their natural energy will come to the fore. A pair with a future, that's for sure!

Feeding for fitness is a subject that has been well covered, but I would just like to mention what I have found successful over many years. We feed alfalfa to all ponies that are working. It provides protein without sugars and also healthy fibre. Even the small, fat ponies are fed it and I have only ever had one pony get laminitis repeatedly. Without strict control of diet versus exercise that pony can go 'off her feet' in days and strangely, she is the slightest built pony we have and she carries no excess flesh at all. Laminitis is also seen in bigger horses. The best way to deal with it is to feed little and often. When the pony is 'sore', box rest with a walk for five munutes twice a day to keep the circulation going and feed just small amounts of alfalfa four times a day until the soreness has eased. The worst thing you can do is to starve the pony as this shuts down the whole metabolism and the problem then takes even longer to control. Keep a balance of exercise versus food to keep laminitis at bay. If you are not going to work the pony for several days then cut back the food intake by at least seventy per cent but still feed alfalfa.

We feed alfalfa and mix twice a day plus haylage, also twice daily, but the performance ponies get haylage three times and an extra 'hard' feed. 'Little and often' may be an old fashioned phrase but it is so true. We find haylage gives a fantastic 'top line' with none of the fat tummy that can be associated with grass and hay. Condition stays on the neck, withers, thighs and loins – in the areas that need to work efficiently. With the alfalfa we use a coarse mix, micronised barley, vegetable oil and additives according to individual needs.

For example, the following are suggested amounts that we use and have great success with. These may not suit all ponies or personal regimes. They are guidelines only.

Competition Pony: 10.3 to 12hh   Stabled/one day in field
(40 to 60 minutes work a day x 6 days a week)

7 am	Lunch	5 pm	9.30 pm
1½ lb alfalfa 1½ lb mix 1 lb micronised barley (depending on condition)	4 lb haylage	as 7 am plus veg oil	6 lb haylage

Competition Cob: 13.3 to 14.2hh   Stabled/one day in field
(40 to 60 minutes work a day x 6 days a week)

7 am	9 am	Lunch	5 pm	9.30 pm
2 lb alfalfa 1¾ lb competition mix 1 lb micronised barley ½ mug Blue Chip Original ½ mug Blue Chip Dynamic	4 lb haylage	4 lb haylage 1½ lb Super Conditioning Flakes	as 7 am plus veg oil	8 lb haylage

This is the maximum we would feed from Week 6 in the fittening programme. Don't feed this amount from Week 1 as you will have a pony fizzing out of his ears!

Horse: 15hh upwards   Stabled/one day in field
(40 to 90 minutes work a day x 6 days a week)

7 am	9 am	Lunch	5 pm	9.30 pm
4 lb alfalfa 3 lb competition mix 1 lb micronised barley ½ mug Blue Chip Original ½ mug Blue Chip Dynamic	6 lb haylage	4 lb haylage 2 lb Super Conditioning Flakes	as 7 am plus veg oil	8 lb haylage

Pleasure Pony: 11 to 14.2hh   Barned/field
(Driven/ridden x 3 days a week)

9 am	5 pm	9.30 pm
3 lb haylage	3 lb haylage	3 to 4lb haylage

In summer (May to Oct) out at night, in during day

If you are competing at National level you must use a guaranteed feed as there are regular random blood tests carried out at events to check for 'forbidden substances'. While the local feed merchant may be very reputable, there could be traces of an unwanted type of feed that has got into the horse mix and will be unacceptable to the rules and regulations governing the sport.

These tables are only guidelines. These amounts work for the horses and ponies in our yard and all the ponies perform well with this routine and maintain fitness and condition throughout the summer when travelling a lot of miles.

Fitness

People sometimes underestimate the fitness that is required for driving and the importance of planning a programme to coincide with competing in an event. It obviously depends on the event – whether you are attending a fun day with your local club and doing pleasure drives, or tackling club/national events with a three section marathon. Do also take into account your own work and personal commitments in relation to how high you want to aim with your pony, it is very time consuming!

I personally don't like to 'rough off' ponies in their down time. I have found that they come back into work more quickly and with less risk of injury if they are rugged and fed all through their break. I believe that their limbs and organs are not put under such strain if they are kept ticking over and warm. I do appreciate that everyone has different circumstances and it is not always possible to follow the 'ideal'. However, consider how hard it is for us to get fit, start running or do gym exercise. It is the same for your pony and much easier to do a little even in 'holiday' time! Loose schooling or lungeing twice a week will 'tick your pony over' and can reduce the weeks required to gain fitness in the spring. Just fifteen minutes is sufficient to keep the muscles in good order.

There are those who believe a total holiday is essential. I agree, but not to the extent of 'close down'. Again, imagine your reaction to having to work again after five months doing nothing, not even household chores! It would be a shock to the system and the brain too; a little discipline and routine makes life much more pleasant for us all, but does not need to be seen as boring.

For pleasure driving and club days, if you drove your pony three to four times a week, doing four to five miles, then it would be realistic to expect a good performance at a club day. This distance on the road is quite easy for the pony; so do try to put in some field work too, to increase fitness.

> **Top Tip:**
> If you practise dressage in an arena of 80 x 40 metres, you only have to go around the outside four times to notch up nearly a kilometre. So not only are you schooling, but also building fitness on grass.

Stanley with his three-phase competition vehicle and happy passengers. Sensible fluorescents but the driver being lazy and not holding her whip!

Suggested fitness regime for club event of 14 kilometres

Week	How Often	Location	Time/Pace	Distance	Comment
1	Min 4 days	Road	Walk	2 – 4 km	Build up to 4 km over the week
2	Min 4 days	Road	Walk Trot	4 km Up to 2 km in 500m sections	Break up your walk distance with trot sections
3	Min 5 days	Field	Walk Trot Overall 30 mins	Gentle schooling in both paces	Consistency of pace is more important than speed
4	Min 5 days	Road or Field	Walk Trot	1 km 8 km	Distance is important – where and how you do it is up to you ie. drive out or schooling
5	6 days	Road or Field	Walk Working Trot	1 km 10 km	Use walk as a breather between trot sections. Practicing a cones course at correct speed is ideal
6	6 days	1 day Road 1 day Road 2 days cones/dressage schooling 1 day field/track 1 day field/track	Walk/Trot Inc. 10 min walk Walk/Trot 40 mins Walk/Trot Walk/Trot Inc. 10 min walk both days	8 km 12 km 8 km @ Sec A speed 12 km @ Sec A speed	Alternate so you and the pony don't get bored
7	6 days	1 day Road 1 day Road 2 days cones/dressage schooling 1 day field/track 1 day field/track	Walk/Trot Inc. 10 min walk both days Walk/Trot 45 mins Trot No walk Trot Trot /Canter	8 km 14 km 8 km @ Sec A speed 6 km @ Sec E speed 2 km Sec A speed	Canter 4 times for a distance of 250 mtrs with 250 mtrs trot in between *(see note 1)*
8	6 days	1 day Road 1 day Road 2 days cones/dressage schooling 1 day field/track 1 day field/track	Trot Trot Inc. 10 mins walk Walk/Trot 45 mins No walk Walk Canter/Trot Walk	8 km 16 km 8 km Sec A speed 1 km 3 km 1 km	Must be no less than 5 days before marathon *(see note 2)* Canter 6 times for a distance of 250 mtrs with 300 mtrs trot in between

Horse speeds:	Section A:	15 km/h
	Walk:	7 km/h
	Section E:	14 km/h
Pony speeds:	Section A:	14 km/h
	Walk:	6 km/h
	Section E:	13 km/h
Club Novice/Small Pony speeds:	Section A:	12 km/h
	Walk:	5 km/h
	Section E:	12 km/h

Note 1:
This simulates the obstacles and gets your pony used to producing a burst of energy at the end of a phase.

Note 2:
It is very important to keep the balance of glycogen and lactic acid correct in order to keep the muscle in top working order. Too much exertion near a marathon date will not give enough time for the carbohydrates in the food to convert the starch which needs to be stored in the liver and muscles before it is converted into glucose.

'Circuit' and 'Interval' training for driving is as important for marathon fitness as it is for event horses in their cross-country phase. Circuit training is a set distance and speed simulating competition conditions. The interval training in canter over a similar distance required for an obstacle will build up a natural ability to produce energy in short spurts without draining the system, thus enabling the pony to continue the competition without stress to the muscles and finishing in good order.

Top Tip:
Drive your car around the field first to get the total distance, do some sums and convert distance into km and check your time/distance chart *(appendices 2 and 3)* to get the times for the field distance.

Above :
Half cup open blinkers.

Left:
Traditional blinkers.

3 Equipment

Introduction

N ow that we have an idea about what goes in front of the carriage, it is time to consider the equipment that we will require. Again I would like to point out that it doesn't have to be prohibitively expensive. In this chapter I have put together guidelines that I have found work with many ponies and clients, plus ideas gained from other horsemen and hours of study and participation.

Bridle

It is vital that a bridle is fitted correctly in order to get the intended action from the bit. Traditionally for driving the noseband is fixed onto the cheek pieces so that when the bridle is fitted and done up there is absolutely no movement of the cheek pieces. However, freedom of the cheek pieces is essential in order for the bit to work freely and effectively in the bars of the mouth. When the cheek is fixed by the noseband, the pressure needed to deliver the same message is considerably more and the bit fails to act in the way in which it was designed. Look at a riding bridle and ask why does that have a separate noseband? It goes back to the theme of clarity and simplicity in everything we do with our ponies. Our expectations are sometimes much higher than our actual ability to make a request to our equines in a way that *they* understand – not *our* perception of their understanding!

Blinkers were an essential in the olden days to protect your pony's eyes from other drivers' whips and thorn bushes. Nowadays, many drivers still prefer them as they help to prevent distractions and aid the pony's concentration. With the demands of sports driving and high levels of performance in obstacles, half cup blinkers are becoming popular. Many ponies both ride and drive these days, so they may find the full blinker quite restricting. Whatever type of blinker you use it must be positioned so that the animal cannot see behind either below or above the blinker. The ideal position of the eye is just above the halfway line. It is also permissible to drive without blinkers at all and some ponies are much happier without them.

Make sure the browband doesn't cut into the pony's ears. Most driving browbands have two slots either side, one for the cheek pieces and one for the throat lash. This allows a 'rosette' to be placed between the straps. It is a metal disc with a metal D on the back, which has the purpose of preventing the browband from moving. Traditionally, owners had their initials or monograms engraved on these. Sometimes I find that I have to extend the browband to fit with more comfort, so I take the rosette off and move the cheek piece into the slot of the throat lash; this gives the extra room required.

The throat lash is designed to keep the bridle on but must not be too tight, as it will restrict the windpipe and cause discomfort when the pony is working in an outline. Equally, if it is too loose then the purpose is defeated as the bridle may slip over the pony's head should he rub or shake his head.

Browband moved into throat lash slot to give more comfort around the ears. Under headcollar also used so that a lead rope can be attached to that and not to the bit.

The noseband, as already mentioned, needs to be independent from the cheek pieces. Quite often there is a strap from the noseband, which fixes into the back of the buckle of the cheek piece and this works well. If not, then buy a riding flash noseband and fit that to the bridle.

Bits and Bitting

This is quite an emotive issue as it can be subject to fashion, tradition and/or common sense! I would like to focus on what is best for your pony.

Newcomers to driving are often led towards 'proper driving bits', the Liverpool being the most common. This is really only applicable if your primary interest is in Private Driving. Comfort for your pony is the priority in Sports Driving.

Many people who have been driving for a few years comment to me that they didn't know they could use riding bits for driving. If your pony goes well when ridden in a snaffle, there is no reason why you can't continue with that when driving. The key is to achieve comfort, control and confidence in order to get the performance and enjoyment that driving can bring. Just because we sit on a large metal object behind the pony, doesn't mean that we forget hand skills and yank on the reins – quite the reverse. What often happens is that a pony leans on the bit because of unyielding contact and tensing of the driver's muscles. This is misinterpreted as the pony being strong when in fact it is because balance is transferred to the forehand and he has learnt to lean on the dead weight at the end of the reins. So a stronger bit is applied and the whole picture is repeated. It takes two to pull and two to have an argument! Actually 'less is more' in most cases in the single and pair classes. A team of four lively horses or ponies may need separate reviewing.

Traditional driving bits – some can be severe and unyielding while others can have more sympathy.

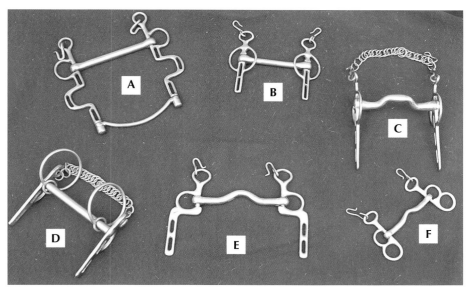

A Buxton with joining bar for pair or team – amazing range of slots for the reins!

B Liverpool with loose cheek, straight bar mouthpiece.

C Liverpool with fixed cheeks and 'correction' mouthpiece – kind on the bars of the mouth and no tongue pressure.

D Swales – very severe.

E Army reversible or elbow – fine on ring but quite severe in slot.

F Butterfly with small port – softer than Liverpool, butterfly cheeks are easier on the pony.

TOP RIGHT:

A Ultra snaffle with rubber covered centre lozenge – helps with teeth grinding and softens the jaw.

B Ultra snaffle with a roller in the lozenge – brilliant for softening and mouthing.

C Double jointed snaffle with cheeks – nice starter bit for young ponies.

D Loose ring correction bit – ideal for a pony that snatches. Very kind position in mouth but stops the 'pull'.

E Eggbutt correction bit – keeps the bit still in the mouth if they have a tendency to chew.

F Double joint of different thicknesses according to the pony's preference! 21mm, 18mm, 16mm.

G Large loose ring double joint – ring gives a little poll pressure.

H Loose ring rubber – ideal starter bit once pony has been mouthed with a key bit.

RIGHT:

A Kimblewick double jointed mouthpiece. Sympathetic – 21mm so quite thick, curb can be used to aid the stopping.

B B bit. Useful if the pony is a bit heavy in the hand or has tongue vices. 16mm mouthpiece.

C Universal – ideal for a strong pony. Dual use – snaffle and then bottom ring to add poll pressure if needed.

D Hanging snaffle – cheeks exert poll pressure and single joint can press into roof of mouth if used with strong pull.

E Butterfly Mullen mouth – a nice bit for a strong pony as shaped mouthpiece lies across the tongue.

For many years I have used double jointed mouthpieces with a variety of ponies. Some have different cheeks, which will influence the effectiveness of the bit. Some have a curb chain to add a little bit more control and pressure, but still allowing the softness and comfort these mouth pieces induce.

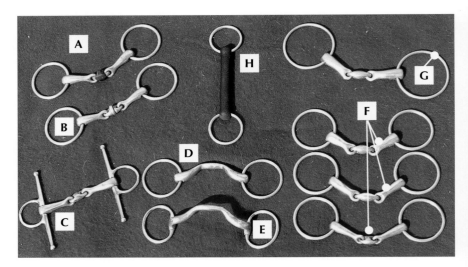

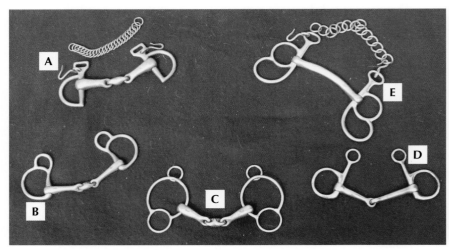

It is imperative that you know the difference between being 'light in the hand' due to correct balance and contact, as opposed to 'light' due to strong bitting making the pony 'back off' the contact, though still looking as if he is in the correct position. I always use a flash noseband. When pressure is applied to the bars, the pony will open his mouth to evade the request and this often results in harsher rein handling. With the mouth closed we can be light in our request and more direct.

ABOVE:
Universal bit with the double-jointed mouthpiece fitted here on the 'snaffle' ring.

ABOVE:
With the rein fitted onto the second ring, the bit can exert some downward pressure on the poll to encourage the pony to slow down and soften.

ABOVE:
Sometimes the pony may evade through his jaw and become strong that way. Try a Grakle noseband as this helps reduce the resistance.

RIGHT:
This shows how the ring can slide through the mouthpiece to increase the poll pressure without harming the bars of the pony's mouth.

A double-jointed bit allows the bars of the mouth to receive separate instructions from each of the driver's hands and therefore they need not apply the same pressure to gain a response. Any mouthpiece with copper or sweet iron encourages the pony to salivate, enabling him to be much more responsive to directions. If the pony dislikes a double joint then do first check that the mouthpiece isn't either too fat, causing discomfort due to filling the mouth, or too thin and exerts too sharp or direct a command. In all the ponies I have schooled and driven, and there have been many, I would say only five per cent won't accept the double joint.

In this case perhaps a Mullen mouthpiece will be more comfortable, the curve sitting slightly above the tongue as opposed to a straight bar which can put pressure on the tongue. Equally, the much used single jointed snaffle is very severe when applied with force as the joint pushes directly up into the roof of the mouth, putting a lot of pressure onto the bars of the mouth. The size of the rings of the snaffle has an effect as well. Larger rings will give some poll pressure, while smaller ones reduce it. If you feel insecure with your riding bit, then do please try to keep it simple. Butterfly cheeks

How the Liverpool lies in the mouth without reins, actually pointing forward.

With rein attached, already exerting pressure before the driver makes his demands.

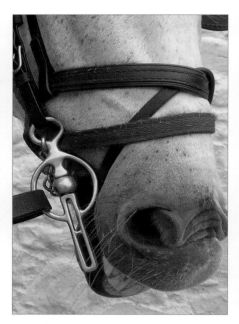

The cheek of the Liverpool twisting and digging into the pony's lips, note his reaction – not impressed! This can happen particularly with pairs.

are kind to the pony. Liverpool cheeks can twist into the side of the mouth, depending on which slot is used for the reins. This can distort the whole message we are trying to get across, particularly when driving a pair.

I personally feel that if you have to drive on the second bar of any driving bit with a tight curb chain, then either the pony is unsuited to the driver or the training is not producing a relaxed and happy pony. Fear and discomfort can also be signs of being strong – check his back and teeth before 'bitting up'. There are no quick fixes so be prepared to accept that 'strong' ponies are a product of strong insensitive hands. No pony is born with a hard mouth; this is what we humans have made it. With negotiation and 'feeling' a pony will get its confidence in the messages you deliver via the reins. Almost every 'strong' pony can be re-educated into a snaffle; it just takes driver confidence and having the will to make 'the difference' to your pony through harmony and understanding. The American Indians used to ride on just a piece of string …

Harness

Choosing the right type of harness for the pony that you have is not too difficult, even though it may look like a bag of knitting gone wrong! Buying a 'leather' harness for £80 is not a bargain, so don't be fooled into thinking so. The stitching can be bad and various parts will pull away as they are not double stitched. You could end up having a nasty accident when the harness is in bits round your pony's legs. The most cost effective harness is the webbing and/or synthetic type. There are many reputable British companies that have the expertise and know-how to produce a worthy harness that's safe and easy to clean. For a new basic synthetic harness for a 12.2 to 13hh pony you should look to spend £275 to £400. This will buy quality and fit (which is crucial) and will last for years. A small pony pairs harness will be £600 to £1000. For cob size and horse pair, due to the extra strong materials required as the power of the animal increases, you will be looking at a minimum of £1500. Don't be talked into considering lightweight/narrow straps for anything over 14hh. The same for single cob/horse – extra width on the breast collar and breeching pays dividends, so around £650 for this size.

Fitting harness to the pony for the first time takes ages, so don't be in a hurry. Most of the time you will be driving in a breast collar – this must be above the point of the shoulder and below the windpipe so that breathing isn't affected.

The neck piece with rein terrets needs to sit about six inches up from the wither and preferably be at least three inches wide, otherwise it can create a pressure point for the pony and be uncomfortable.

A consideration
In ridden dressage snaffles are compulsory at Preliminary and Novice level and permitted up to Advanced. In eventing, snaffles can be used up to Senior FEI three day event level. Maybe we should all absorb this and think why …? Does the welfare of the pony spring to mind …? And the desire to become knowledgeable horsemen and not letting metal work dictate outline …?

PARTS OF THE HARNESS

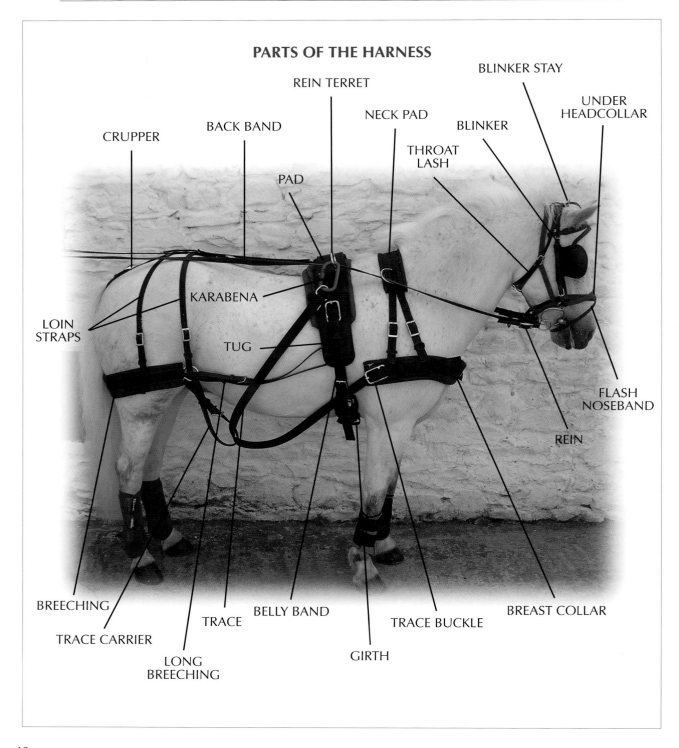

CRUPPER

BACK BAND

PAD

REIN TERRET

NECK PAD

THROAT LASH

BLINKER STAY

BLINKER

UNDER HEADCOLLAR

LOIN STRAPS

KARABENA

TUG

FLASH NOSEBAND

REIN

BREECHING

TRACE CARRIER

LONG BREECHING

TRACE

BELLY BAND

GIRTH

TRACE BUCKLE

BREAST COLLAR

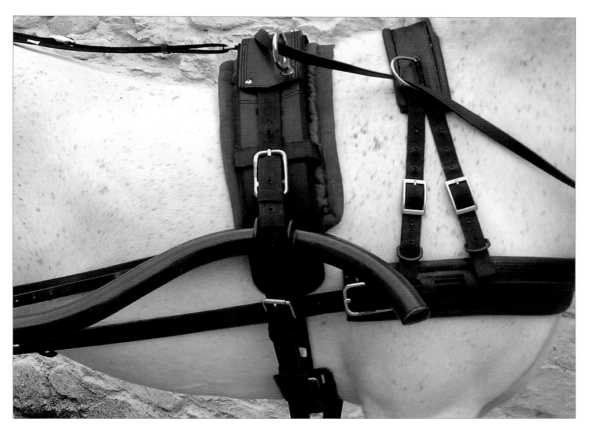

The saddle or pad sits behind the wither with the girth done up evenly each side. The belly band, which has the tugs attached, should be buckled loosely until the carriage is being put to.

  The crupper comes from the back of the pad to under the tail. The tautness of this is crucial – too slack and the whole thing slides off the pony's back, too tight and it will be desperately uncomfortable. When correctly fitted your hand should slip under nicely, giving about four inches between the pony's back and crupper at the point behind the pad. Another way to tell is to lift the tail, if there is a gap of two to three inches from the crupper to the pony's dock then that is also all right.

  Trace length is sorted when fitting the pony into the carriage, but before you put the pony in, clip the trace ends back to either breeching rings or rein terrets for safety. We also have karabenas on every trace end or quick release clips, as this is far safer than the slot end to get off quickly if needs be. The traditional way is to roll them up, but it is not always practical to do this. When the tug is sitting in the middle of the pad there must be four inches of free space so you can slide your hand between the back of his thigh and the

ABOVE:
Tug placing in centre of pad. For fixed shafts you need a sliding back band as above.

ABOVE:
Breast collar sitting above point of shoulder and below windpipe.

breeching. The breeching straps can simply hang down if you choose to attach to the shaft. I have chosen to use the old fashioned 'trade' way of breeching. That is, from the breeching ring along the back of the tug, back through it and buckled up. The reasoning hehind long breechng is to give more freedom for the pony's loins and lateral movement. When the breeching is fastened to the shaft the pony has no more than four inches of movement within the straps, which limits his athletic ability. We are constantly looking to improve bend and elasticity for all phases but fixing his quarters to two 'metal poles' does not make this easy. Hence taking the breeching forward allows total freedom to move laterally and engage the back end with no restrictions. The control of the vehicle is the same with both types of breeching. I drive many turnouts and formations daily and have never experienced a problem with this. Many people have not been exposed to this way and I think they should try new ideas to find out the benefits.

When harnessing a single pony both reins must be attached before putting to – feed them through the rein terrets on the pad first, then the rings on the neck and onto the bit. Secure the driver's end of the reins either through the rein terret or the back strap (crupper strap).

ABOVE AND RIGHT:
Fitting the crupper. Note the cable tie from the ring down to the tug, a quick way to hold the back band from sliding when using independent shafts.

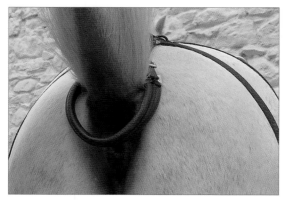

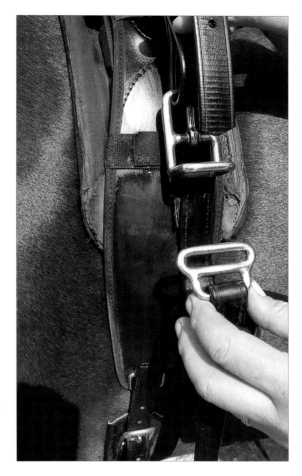
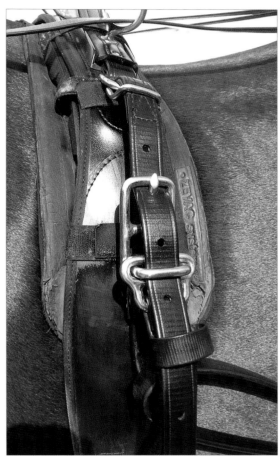

Quick release tug – an excellent idea. Useful for shaft ends that have a loop or for the double tug stop. Showing here how the lower piece of the tug slots over the extension on the buckle and the tug strap slots in to prevent the metal parts coming adrift.

Long breeching from the breeching ring through the tug.

As the long breeching looks with the shaft.

Traditional breeching attached to the D ring on the shaft.

An 'empathy' breast collar. Designed to spread the 'pull' area, half way between a breast collar and a full collar. Short shafts with a quick release tug and reins at a good angle to the driver.

A Tilbury tug on a short shaft showing how it wraps round and holds the shaft in place.

Top Tip:
It is advisable to leave your headcollar on at all times when driving. There are some good 'under headcollars' available which don't have cumbersome buckles. This is a safety factor – your groom has a place to fix the rope other than the bit. When putting on the bridle, the pony is less likely to escape if you don't have to undo anything.

The bridle always goes on last and comes off first (once the pony is out of the shafts!) Make sure your throat lash is on the outside of the headcollar and that the noseband sits inside the headcollar so as not to cause pressure points when it is tightened up.

The reins need to have at least two holes at the bit end. Only use the first one, so that you have a spare hole in case of wear or accidental tear. Should your rein billet be such that there is a long gap from the bit to the hole, then tape the buckle for safety. This prevents it from moving or getting caught on the bit, especially with a Liverpool and butterfly cheek.

We are almost ready, apart from crash hats for the driver and crew and boots all round for the pony. Many drivers would not be seen in public with a booted pony, but mine never leave the yard without! As with ridden animals front boots protect from knocks, and back boots can prevent horrific damage to tendons if you have an

ABOVE LEFT:
A good type of driving under headcollar with no buckles to get in the way.

ABOVE RIGHT:
Throat lash fastened on the outside of the headcollar. Bridle noseband sitting close to the pony with the headcollar's noseband clearly over the top.

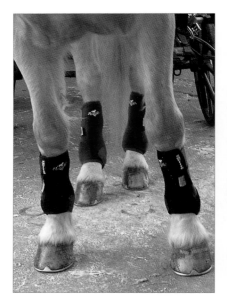 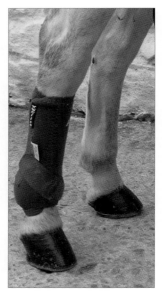 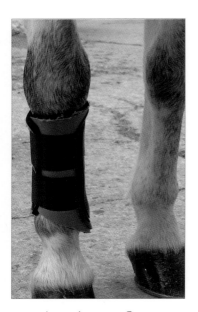

accident. I have had boots shredded when a pony has bucked, got a leg over a trace or shaft and kicked like mad. If the carriage tips up, it's the back legs that are vulnerable. I have also seen several ponies with severe tendon injuries after accidents because they were not protected by boots. Please don't take the chance that it won't happen to your pony. New boots are cheaper than a new pony.

Finally, before we head for the carriage, put on a fluorescent tabard and front boots with a reflective material are a good idea.

ABOVE LEFT AND CENTRE:
Tendon and fetlock protection with an 'impact absorbing' boot.

ABOVE RIGHT:
A good fitting boot with protection down the inside of the cannon bone and fetlock joint.

Top Tip:
Crash hats: A high proportion of people driving carriages do so without crash hats. In the showing world you never see a crash hat – only toppers and fancy creations for the ladies; the same in the dressage phase of driving trials. Crash hats are compulsory for the marathon phase but you frequently see them hanging on the carriage before the start and immediately after the finish. When I first started driving I too never thought to wear a hat, but I would never have dreamt of getting on a horse without one. I was quickly corrected by a friend who pointed out the dangers, thank goodness! I have had some spectacular accidents and would not be as fit as I am if I hadn't had head protection. DON'T take a chance. Accidents happen to the safest of people and especially on the road where we have no control over speeding or discourteous drivers. Vanity is a price too high to pay for sanity.

Putting To a Single Turnout

Ensure the reins are looped through the offside terret and the belly band is loose ready to bring the shafts forward to the pony and into the tugs. Your groom should be at your horse's head during the procedure.

Never back your pony into the shafts and always put a hand on the pony's rump as you bring the shafts forward so he knows what you are doing. Slide the shaft through the tug until you get to the tug stop, always making sure that your tug rests in front of the tug stop, *never* behind it. Next, take your traces and attach them to the swingle tree if you are using a breast collar. Often for more formal occasions you will be using a full traditional collar, in which case the traces must be attached to the shaft hooks. Check that the traces are straight with no twists that may chafe the pony. Do up the belly band sufficiently tight to hold the shafts in place, but not so tight that it acts as a second girth.

It is imperative that you then re-check from the front that all necessary straps and buckles are done up. We start with the bridle, ensuring that the pin of the buckle is actually in the rein hole where it should be and that the billet end is through the keeper. The reins should be going through both rein terrets on the neck strap and pad. The tug should be in the correct place with girth and belly band secure and the trace is firmly attached to the swingle tree (i.e. make sure quick releases are properly closed or the loop goes right around the pig end on the swingle tree). Remember the other side as well!

Mount the vehicle from the offside taking the reins from the terret to the vehicle and then climb in seating yourself onto the 'box seat'. Make sure you have your reins sorted and you are in control of the pony before your groom releases the lead rope and their position; the groom can then mount the vehicle once you have given the instruction.

Passengers must not mount the vehicle before the driver is in place, nor must the driver dismount the vehicle leaving passengers still aboard.

Whip

A whip should be carried at all times in the right hand; it is basically 'the riding legs' of the turnout. You can use it as a directional aid or for more impulsion. It is also useful to help correct faults that creep in now and again. The most simple guide as to the size of whip required is to remember that the driver needs to be able to reach the shoulder of the pony without leaning so far forward that their balance is impaired.

When I coach people new to the sport, we use a short stemmed whip with a short lash as this builds up the muscle in the lower arm. It gets the driver used to holding the whip and learning its control without constantly bashing the pony on the bottom or inadvertently tickling him. If you drive a tandem or team, the thong of the whip must be able to make contact with the lead pony. When holding the whip it needs to sit at an angle of ten to ten while not in use.

Young driver showing the correct angle at which the whip should be carried and nicely level hands.

To use the whip when driving one handed, just move your right arm forward and apply stroking movements with the thong; use your thumb to roll the stem of the whip. Occasionally it is necessary to really flick it to make a definite contact with the sides or shoulder of the pony. Always bear in mind that it's there as an *aid* to encourage or correct, not as a punishment. Your voice tone is the punishment.

Traditionalists of the coachman style of driving always say that you cannot use the whip efficiently without losing rein contact when driving two handed. That is not the case and there are two ways:

1. For a general encouragement aid, the right hand tips forward taking the whip from the 'ten to ten' angle to lower and forward. The right rein is tightened as the hand tips forward, while the wrist rotates left or right according to the side the driver wishes to place the whip on.

2. If you need to use the whip forward of the pad then a 'half bridge'; of the reins is needed. Both hands stay on the reins; the right rein is secured under the left thumb while the right hand and whip slide down the right rein into the position whereby the whip can be applied to the shoulder. When mastered, you will never have slack in your reins at any time and you will be able to put your whip exactly where you need it.

Once you are fully competent, then the reins can be used in the continental one-handed fashion with the whip hand free to move.

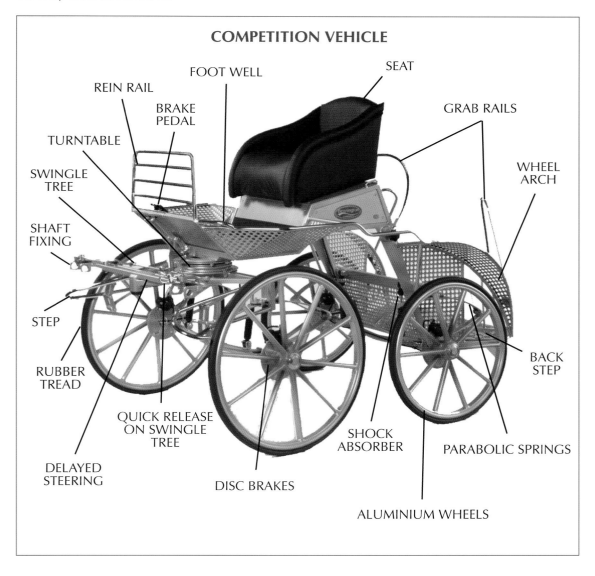

COMPETITION VEHICLE

Vehicles

A good example of a 'cheap' exercise vehicle and its faults. There is no tug stop and the swingle tree is mounted far too high for the size of pony for which the vehicle is intended. There is also no shape to the shaft ends.

Your choice of vehicle is such an important decision as it can really affect your pleasure and confidence. Cheap is not always best and thinking you have a bargain by getting a £200 exercise cart out of a catalogue or a market only to discover there are no tug straps and the swingle tree is in the wrong place. You may unwittingly end up with a disaster despite the best intentions. Again, you need to assess your ambitions. Are you opting to drive for pleasure and have fun days within your local area? Do you drive on your own or with friends/family?

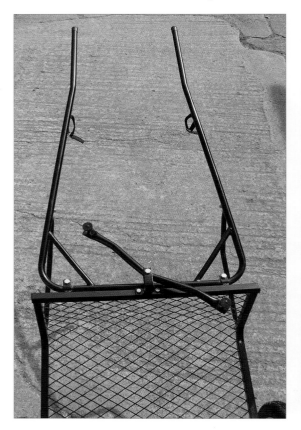 

A two-wheel vehicle to start with is very versatile as you can take part in club and indoor events with these, as well as dressage at national level. If you do have to exercise your pony on your own, you are much safer than in a four-wheeler. It is possible to balance the vehicle and most are easy to get out of if you need to get to the pony's head in a hurry. Many basic two-wheelers can be dismantled to fit into a trailer or boot of a car, which makes it easier to get to pleasure events and club competitions. Getting out and about is key to your enjoyment, sense of achievement and a reward for all the dedication one has to have with ponies in the first place.

Perhaps you should be a little choosy as to which type of two-wheeler you decide on. A really basic one as previously mentioned may not be of the best design for the pony. The design of the shafts can determine how well the pony turns. If the shafts are very straight from the carriage forward, this can restrict the pony so much that they become very stiff in the way they go. Whereas shaped shafts give a little more freedom through the shoulder and back; resistance through the loins is therefore lessened. Also if the end of the shaft is turned out and downwards (often called a 'swan neck') it doesn't press onto the shoulder when turning. This is very important for obstacle driving when you are hoping for tight turns.

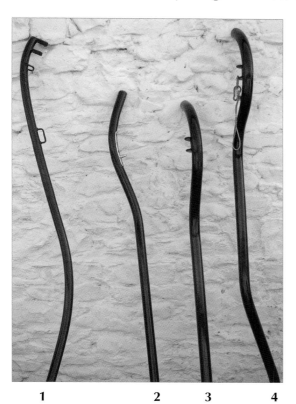

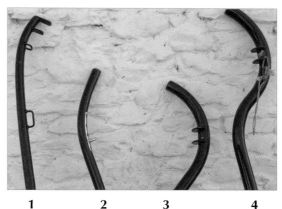

1   2   3   4   1   2   3   4

ABOVE AND RIGHT:

1 A short shaft that stops at the pad can be very effective for marathon driving as there is total shoulder freedom. Note the loop on the shaft behind the double tug stop, this is to attach a strap that goes behind and through the tug to hold the shaft in place. Only suitable for four-wheelers.

2 Traditional shaft with a small tug stop. Not safe for cross-country driving as the tug can bounce over the stop. Even with Tilbury tugs that wrap tightly to the shaft you are inviting a problem.

3 A 'swan neck' shaft with a double-sided tug stop. Very safe and a super shape for freedom of the shoulder.

4 The 'Z' shaft from Bennington is a sympathetic design for marathon driving, giving freedom for the horse to move and less opportunity to get a leg over the shaft. Note the clip and line from the tug stop which clips onto the rein terret, again for safety.

How the sport has changed since 1983! Michael Mart and daughter Sue competing at Osberton with a two-wheeler. No crash hats or boots on the pony and spectators wandering along the track. Health and Safety would have a field day now!

Do also look at the tug stops. These are vital to prevent the tug sliding back down the shaft towards the carriage. If they do and the carriage touches the pony, it can cause a nasty accident. For Sports Driving when we are being quite athletic with the vehicle and pony, we need more support than if driving sedately around the roads or in a show ring. The most secure is the double tug stop, which reduces the chance of a mishap. The belly band done up in the correct position will help hold the tug in place and prevent too much bouncing in the shafts.

FAR RIGHT:
Double tug stop with tug in correct position on the pad.

RIGHT:
A: *Traditional tug stop and long straight shaft end.*

B: *Competition swan neck shaft with double tug stop.*

The balance of a two-wheeler is very important. When sitting in the vehicle with your groom, the weight of the shafts pressing down on to the tugs must be 'finger light'. There should be no pressure or weight onto the pad. The same applies if you are driving alone, make sure it is not 'floating' if you have previously balanced the vehicle for a passenger. The way to balance is to move your seat forward or back according to the 'load' of passengers.

Balance and fitting correct for a two-wheeler with groom. Note the rein contact, consistent and very straight to the bit, enabling clear instructions.

A lovely picture of happiness (and amazement from the sheep!) Everything is spot on with this turnout. Whip is correct, legs apart to balance the carriage with the driver in the middle of the seat. Carriage fits correctly to the pony and at the right height.

A brilliant new design of 'two' wheel vehicle is the Bennington 'Fun Bug'. The principle is that of a two-wheeler, but it has a double axle of pneumatic tyres, which results in perfect balance and no weight on the pony. It is very comfortable and extremely safe in its design detail with extras, which can take you into club Pre Novice, Novice and Junior classes; and it can legally be towed behind a car! I would strongly recommend this type of vehicle, as it will always have a use even when you move on to a four-wheeler.

Another factor to take into account is the type of tyres – solid rubber tyres or pneumatics. If you exercise on wet ground pneumatics make it much easier on the pony as you won't sink in so much, but at club level they are only accepted in Novice classes or fun days. In the show ring they would come under 'exercise vehicles'. The solid rubber tyre has no exclusions. The only type of wheel/tyre to avoid is the bicycle type as they are liable to bend under stress. I don't think there is an advantage over either tyre, and it is your personal choice, but do remember that you can get punctures with pneumatics and I have had strange looks when popping into a garage to pump up my tyres, and even worse if the pony does a dropping!

BELOW LEFT:
Fun Bug – easy to get in and out and no 'spokes' to get caught in and easy for a small pony to pull.

BELOW RIGHT:
Fun Bug – with a back step for Novice club marathon or extra passengers.

Four-wheelers can change your driving quite a bit and, in a way, they give you more freedom and excitement. The turntable makes all manoeuvring so much easier for your pony and less restricting for his flexibility. He will now be able to turn tight corners without having to cross over his legs to push the carriage as it will follow him and he can get more back-end engagement. There are many types available, some designed specifically for dressage and cones, known as 'presentation' vehicles; some designed just for the marathon phase. Others are designed for all three phases, which are the most popular. Then there are a host more for pleasure driving. I think the key points to remember when looking for a four-wheeler are:

1. Driving position – if the seat is too far back off the front axle it can be unstable during the marathon on rough or undulating

terrain, due to too much weight towards the back axle. The front axle will lift off the ground and you feel as if you have no steering.

2. The position of the groom's seat for the dressage and cones – you often see vehicles with the 'dicky' seat almost hanging off the back step so that the groom's weight bounces. This again makes the front axle lift or be very light, which reduces the effectiveness of the positioning of the carriage. Sitting sideways can also alter the balance of the vehicle jeopardising its stability and therefore the confidence of the driver. The best position is seated directly behind the driver facing either forward or backwards. If the driver is on a box seat sitting to the right of the vehicle, then the groom can sit sideways on the left as this will balance the load.

The Bennington XL carriage in action.

The Bennington XL – a lovely specialist vehicle for the marathon.

Fun Bug in the dressage phase with the groom holding a second pair of reins as the driver is only seven years old. (Note the pony is wearing boots. This is a local rule to Scottish Club events. There are no penalties for this and you can go straight on to the cones phase.)

Well balanced for the dressage and cones.

3. Leg room for the driver and seat angle – the seat needs to be long enough to support your legs and deep enough to hold you when going fast on the marathon. Your legs need to reach the front foot well and be able to brace you into the seat. If the seat is too far back and your feet only just touch the front, you may be fine for dressage and cones but not braced enough for rough terrain. If your knees are too bent, then firstly it will look awful for your dressage and, secondly, you will be very uncomfortable for longer periods of driving.

4. Cost! Unfortunately it always comes into the equation. We do have some excellent carriage builders in Britain with skilled craftsmen ensuring the vehicle is built to last and to high safety standards. There are also many imported vehicles with a more attractive price tag. Many thousands of these vehicles are used daily and perform to the standards required, though they may need a small amount of alteration to suit your requirements. Long term, most British made vehicles will hold their price and performance.

Whatever you drive, maintenance is a crucial part of your routine. Check the vehicle regularly, noticing if something is starting to wear or needs greasing. This will help to make your driving safer.

Bear these wheel widths (RIGHT) in mind when buying your vehicle, especially a three-phase one as you will need to have an extending rear axle. Most club events will accommodate your two-wheel vehicle at 125 cm up to Novice level, after that 138 cm is preferred. Hoola hoops to extend the axles are no longer permitted.

If you choose to add a presentation vehicle for dressage and cones to your now expanding fleet, the axle width should be set at the appropriate measurement for your class. The front and rear axle both being the same width makes driving cones slightly easier.

Fitting the Carriage

Don't underestimate the time required in the beginning to set up the carriage, harness and pony correctly. It will be time well spent. The shafts, whether in a two- or four-wheeler, need to be sitting approximately half way up the pony's side. In a two-wheeler the shafts need to sit level with the carriage. If the carriage is tipping back there are two likely reasons for this – (1) the tugs are too high; (2) the carriage is too small. Wheel size increases the height of the vehicle, so if you have 23 inch wheels it won't fit a 15hh horse – although it might if it's a four-wheeler, but I'll come to that.

The 'balance' needs to be checked as discussed earlier. The distance from the back of the pony to the swingle tree and splashboard is very important. The pony must not be able to touch

Top Tip: Wheel widths required in competition

Marathon wheel width for every class 125 cm

Single Pony/Horse dressage and cone wheel width 138 cm

Pony Pair dressage and cone wheel width 138 cm

Horse Pair dressage and cone wheel width 148 cm

Pony Team dressage and cone wheel width 138 cm

Horse Team dressage and cone wheel width 158 cm

RIGHT:
A Spider Phaeton for a
horse pair.

BELOW:
Ann Gilbert driving a
lovely pair of ponies to a
smart presentation vehicle.
Well matched and
balanced.

the swingle with his legs when braking the vehicle as this could give him a fright. Equally, having the splashboard touching his behind when going down hill could be interesting. Personally, I like at least 18 inches from both as I do tend to drive with the pony quite far from the carriage, as I feel happier. It's not funny when the pony bucks and he's close enough to land in the foot well. Don't on the other hand have the pony so far off the rein rail that you need extensions to your arms.

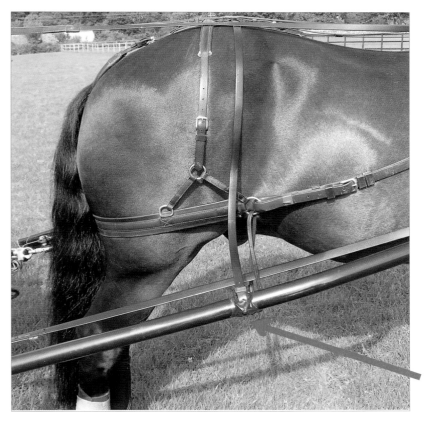

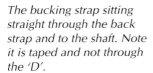

The bucking strap sitting straight through the back strap and to the shaft. Note it is taped and not through the 'D'.

View from the box seat, the bucking strap with enough slack to allow back end engagement in work.

Fitting a four-wheeler is the same with regard to the pony's distance from the carriage. The shafts also need to lie in the same position, but may well come up from the vehicle at different angles. The balance of the vehicle on four wheels takes any pressure off the shafts, so the tug is just there to hold them in place with the belly band tightened to prevent it flapping off the pony's sides. Should the belly band be too loose then, as you drive in trot, the vehicle weaves from side to side and you will soon realise your mistake!

Now we are kitted out and ready to go – so what's next?

4 Technique and Schooling

Our method of communication with our pony needs to be clear and concise. We do not need strength and force to drive. To create a harmonious partnership we need to communicate through our minds and bodies with clear instructions. It is so true when one hears people say 'what's in the brain; goes down the rein!' Few of us appreciate how subtle and how little can achieve so much until we try. I'm not suggesting that we tiptoe around our ponies saying 'pretty please' and drive with flapping reins. To the contrary! *Negotiation* is the skill we need; domination will not achieve a happy partnership in the long term, nor will being too soft. This means 'talking' to your pony in a language he understands. It is not a case of power and dominance – or of punishment if they fail to cooperate with any 'demands' you make on them.

It's all very well saying this, but how do we actually achieve it?

Firstly, we have to accept that the directions and indications we give to our equine partner will result in how they go (apart from obvious outside surprises!) They are a reflection of you. If you spectate at an event there are always one or two turnouts that look exceptional, with no hint of evasion, stiffness or wrong bend. Why is this? Because the driver will be relaxed and following where he needs to go, looking forward and planning the next move. As a result the pony feels confident about what is expected of him. It won't have been an easy road to attain that level, but the driver will have achieved clarity in his directions and aids to correct any evasions early on so they don't become established. Don't think when you have overcome one issue that there won't be more; there will be and when you move on to pairs or teams it will be double or quadruple the challenge!

The voice is absolutely vital in driving – its importance is on a par with legs when riding. It isn't so much what you say, as how you say it – intonation is the key to your pony's understanding. When actually asking for a movement or transition, make sure it is a clear message. I often liken it to a small child learning to read – you start off with large letters in a simple font to avoid confusion. For example, if you are out with a friend catching up on gossip, how on earth can your pony define the difference between the 'latest fashion' and 'trot on' if you haven't stopped to draw breath to say his name and give the command in a different tone?

Using the pony's name every time before you need his attention for an upward transition will make him alert and quick to respond. Try it with a group of friends, call someone's name and watch the reaction (forget the 'trot on' bit or they will think you have flipped!). Then just chat and in the same tone ask a question within the conversation – see how many react and how quickly! As you now have your pony's attention by saying his name, be quick to follow on with your request and put energy into what you are saying; this will reflect the type of transition you get. 'Troooot-ooooooon' in a flat tone will get a long slow transition, whereas a bright and crisp 'trot on' will energise your pony into a transition exactly when you want it.

For slowing down we need to have a calming tone of voice before any hand aid is necessary. The less pull on the reins the better, we may need that later if the pony gets a fright or is too lively at a show. When we want to calm a person down we don't shout at them as that has the adverse effect. Similarly if we use the pony's name followed by a crisp command to walk or halt, he is going to be utterly confused as he doesn't have the command of language that we do. He thinks the use of his name means he is to be sharp and attentive; so we'll have to change our voice tone and elongate the words. We always use 'whoa' to indicate something is going to change, followed by 'waaalk' or 'staaannd' with a light squeeze of the rein. Give him a fraction of a second to do what you have asked without applying the pressure constantly. If you also relax into the transition it makes it so much easier for your pony. Let your shoulders relax towards your waist and unclench your buttocks so that you allow your waist to drop and then the transition happens with no restrictions from you. The longer you pull back on the reins with constant pressure, the longer the transition takes, which then makes the driver pull the reins harder, irritates the pony and makes him lean on your hand. The next minute you will be saying that your pony is too strong! It's a full circle. If you had taken two seconds to let the pony think about what you asked verbally and then indicated with your hands, he would have done his transition with no bother.

Learning the coordination of the 'squeeze of the rein' and relaxing is a challenge. Similarly, showing a pony who has always pulled like a train that he no longer needs to, takes time and patience.

One of the good things about Sports Driving is that there is no right or wrong way, according to the rules about how you hold your reins. Everyone has their own preference and, as long as you respect that, and the result is the correct way of going, then that is fine. If someone does pass comment on your two-handed driving, just point out that horses have been ridden for thousands of years with two hands – successfully! Ridden dressage is two handed, right up to Grand Prix level.

I personally prefer to hold the reins as if I was riding, but with my little finger inside the rein – the old fashioned way of using the

Top Tip:
'Squeezing the rein' is tightening the grip with the little finger; liken it to squeezing a sponge dry. When the pony has reacted to your request then just relax your grip on 'the sponge' but don't let your hand move forward, as this is then indicating you want him to continue at the previous speed.

bradoon rein of a double bridle. The reason being that the outside of the hand is weathered and you have much more capability to negotiate with the rein using the little finger to tighten or loosen the contact according to the response needed. This helps reduce the number of times you have to shorten the rein. The less 'faffing' on the reins, the clearer the message and the better result you achieve.

In order to be accurate with the signal you give the pony it is vital that the rein is constant through your hand to his mouth. When doing your dressage schooling, if there is slack in the rein and you start 'squeezing' the rein will 'snap' on and off at his mouth and won't give him any idea of what you want. It will also be very uncomfortable. 'Contact' is the feel to his mouth, the weight in your hand. Ideally we want about 2 ounces, any less and the pony is avoiding the contact. Quite often when they are leaning on your hand or evading, or stiff, we can have up to 8 ounces of weight. This then needs to be 'asked' down towards the 2 ounce mark (and it won't happen in one go). Do please be careful not to tense the muscles in the wrist and elbow when squeezing. Get a rhythm from the shoulder to the mouth without getting 'snap'. The easiest way is to think of the rein as a thick piece of elastic going through his mouth up your sleeve, around the back of your neck and down the other sleeve. As you asked your pony to work onto the bit, we need to make sure he doesn't think your hand signals are to slow him down, so we need to keep him forward into the pace by keeping the impulsion. This is where your voice is the aid. Energise the command and repeat the pace word like a metronome so the pony can match his stride to that. It is so important to keep the pace in walk or slow trot while learning to get your pony on the bit. From his perspective,

ABOVE LEFT:
'Riding Style' – gives good grip. Rein coming from base of hand to thumb allows negotiation through the fingers.

ABOVE RIGHT:
'Variation'– rein coming to thumb first. Grip and direction all coming from one place.

he has to use different muscles, which take a while to build up, and slow work is the fastest way to do this. It is easier to go faster over a distance than to have slow muscle control over the same distance with the quarters totally engaged and the pony on the bit without rushing on or leaning on your hand.

I work all our ponies on a gently sloping field as this helps to build muscle control for both up and down hill. Realistically, few of us have perfectly flat fields and many club events are put on thanks to the generosity of local farmers where a perfect flat dressage arena may not be available. If your pony is used to keeping his balance and rhythm on all types of gradient, you are likely to gain a few points.

Top Tip:
Hand Position: we need a constant line from the mouth through the rein terrets, through the base of the hand, along under the arm to the elbow. The elbow needs to rest lightly by the hip. The hands need to be 8 to 9 inches apart. Think of holding a small tray of drinks – your shoulders and waist can turn without spilling the drinks but if you try to alter the level of your hands, then everything falls off the tray!

Note position of hands – 8 inches apart and relaxed elbow at hip.

Our hands must be aware of different terrains, so that we can at all times have the elasticity needed for the pony's confidence and the ability to move from the shoulder to absorb the different rein lengths required. For uphill we need to let our hands and shoulders move forward a little in order for the outline to go longer as the quarters come under the pony further to get the 'push' required to pull the carriage. The rump goes lower and flatter as the hill increases in steepness. The tone of his hind feet on the tarmac changes to a deeper 'clop' the harder he works. Coming down the slope our hands will need to slide back a little to take the slack as the pony will naturally shorten his stride to 'hold' the weight of the carriage. Because his stride length is shorter, the tone of his hind feet is lighter and is more of a 'clip'. Listening to your pony's feet on the road is a great indicator of rhythm, balance and speed. This will then help your work in the field, as you will have heard what you see and now have to feel what you see. Watch how taut or loose your traces are as this indicates whether your pony is working (in draught) or whether the weight of the carriage is pushing onto him – i.e. traces slack.

The key to your dressage is to be able to have the balance through muscle tone and negotiation skills to get the consistent pace and smoothness that looks so natural.

Long Rein Schooling

It is imperative that Sports Driving is not seen to be vastly different from riding. So often I get the comments 'but the pony is so far away' or 'I don't feel in control sitting here!' To be honest, if you and the pony don't speak the same 'language' it doesn't matter where you sit. As we have already said, the basics needed for driving are very similar to those for riding – rein handling, voice and sensitivity plus engagement of the quarters.

To get the feel of 'distance' and control you need to practise long reining. It is an excellent way to cement the commands and get used to controlling the animal in a different manner. You will need a long lunge line (approx 24 to 28 feet long) with a clip at both ends, also a lunge pad or the pad from your harness with the tugs and belly band done up tight. The reins need to come either through the tugs or rings on your roller pad two thirds of the way down his side. The reasoning behind this is that you then have the reins at a consistent angle to your hand when you are on the ground.

One quite often sees ponies being lunged from the top rein terrets which, while not correct, is doing a different job from the one we want to do. This will give a very angled rein as seen above diluting the subtlety of the contact that we want to establish.

With the reins through the roller pad rings onto the bit and coming behind the pony into your hands, hold them as you would

Lungeing pad in position. Here I have extended the ring lower down the pad and fixed a strap each side of the ring under the tummy to stop it from coming up. This will help stop the outside rein from sliding up when lungeing with the two reins.

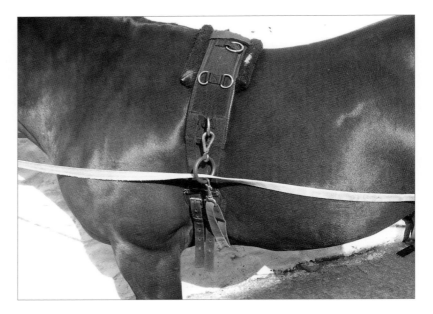

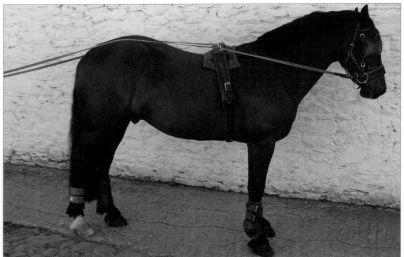

Very angled rein.

your riding reins, but do make sure that the rein is on the outside of your hand, not between the third and fourth fingers.

Start off on the straight as you will need to get the feel of the rein contact and watch for any slackness. At this stage it is very important to feel the pony's mouth and mirror his movement through your shoulders, not by twisting your arm out, down or into your tummy. The easiest and most comfortable way to turn your pony is to mirror the movement with your body as you ask for it. Doing this prevents the pull and yank, therefore creating a smooth and easy turn. On the long reins it is easy to see when the contact is irregular.

Once you are happy turning corners and doing deviations, take yourself to a line of five cones placed about 8 metres apart. Bend the pony up the line in walk, turn at the top and bend back down again. The turn at the top is going to be the challenge. If you are turning to the right, for example, it is not practical to run behind the pony to get the turn, so we have to take a loop of the inside rein to bring the pony around tightly. Allow the left arm to extend from the shoulder in order for the pony to get maximum freedom on the outside. As the pony comes round and towards the next cone we have to ease the

BELOW :
Prince going onto his forehand and not 'using' himself.

LEFT:
Here on the circle there is a good change in outline and activity from behind. He is also much more towards 'self carriage'.

loop out of the hand at the same time as bringing our left shoulder back in line, the right hand then easing forward and the left hand/shoulder coming back to make the turn round the second cone. If you don't keep the contact then your pony will bob and weave everywhere except round the cones.

ABOVE:
Loop has been taken and the right turn is commencing.

ABOVE RIGHT:
Loop clearly visible in right hand and about to be released as the turn is completed.

Take a right loop by bringing your left hand across onto the right rein about 4 inches in front of the right hand and then take your right hand under the rein to in front of the left hand and take hold of the right rein between thumb and forefinger, then the left hand returns to position leaving a 'loop' in the rein which has shortened the inside rein considerably to enable the turn. Let the loop slide through your thumb to reduce the size of the turn and return to straight line. The actual process should just take fractions of a second and there is no loss of contact on either rein when executed properly. Reverse the procedure for a left turn.

As you become comfortable with the turn and contact, put yourself and pony onto a circle but letting out the outside rein and shortening the inside rein. Lungeing with long reins is the most efficient way to teach your pony balance and going on the bit. It also improves the driver's sympathy and understanding as to what happens with 'an outline' and what it looks like when right, or when improvements are needed.

Demonstrating taking a left loop.

1 – taking right hand across to maintain contact on rein whilst left hand …

2 – drops under the supported left rein to take the 'loop' …

3 – and the right hand can continue as usual …

Changing from a left turn to the right. Prince has good lateral bend to the right.

Straightening Prince up as he passes the cone before he has to swing right and then left.

There is nothing more pleasing than working your equine in the simplest of bits to get a result. It won't happen overnight and if you don't have the tenacity to work with 'nature', then there are plenty of 'quick fixes' available, but they will not be discussed here, as I don't believe a pony should ever need any gadget to force it into the shape we want.

There are so many 'quick fixes' on the market but not one of them will give a natural balanced outline with the full cooperation of the pony in spite of what the instructions may say. The only way is to show the pony what you want and allow him to discover the 'how', then when he has understood for himself it is learned for life – and in a snaffle too! Once you start with gadgets your pony will submit, but quickly revert to the original way of going once they are taken off, because he has been tricked into an outline and has not learned to accept it naturally. It is a bit like using 'Easy Start' on an engine, a quick fix, when it would have been better if the initial problem had been sorted!

So how are we going to get this outline when standing on the ground with two long reins? Negotiate! The outside rein is the one controlling the pace, size of circle and bend. The inside rein indicates the direction and asks for submission through the jaw. Don't set the outside rein, allow a weight of about 4 ounces and squeeze your little finger like a pulse every three or four strides, this will prevent the pony leaning onto your hand. The inside rein will need to 'pulse' quite fast in order for the pony to accept the bit and soften his jaw. You may have up to 8 to 9 ounces of 'weight' on the rein to start with but this can comes as light as 1 or 2 ounces with the negotiation. When pulsing the little fingers, don't let your hand turn in, up or out or anywhere other than in line with rein to mouth. If you need more space to shorten or lengthen, then move from the shoulder. Your wrist and elbow must not restrict the movement in any way.

The minute you start to set your muscles against the pony, he will do the same. The simplest way to think of all commands to the pony is through body language – over 90 per cent of human communication is non verbal – and we can talk as well! So please remember, when your pony is not responding to your request, it is probably because you are making demands too complicated for him to understand and shouting at him or getting cross is going to exacerbate the issue. Go right back to the beginning and start again in 'capital letters' with a smile and have the patience to explain as if he were a toddler!

The consistency of rein contact is crucial to the success of the request for softening onto the bit. Should you get any slack or snatch on the rein, however small, this is going to magnify to the mouth and reduce the cooperation. The mouth should be very wet once acceptance has begun and slowly you will be able to ease your hand towards the pony and he will stay in the outline or lengthen downwards and as you pick up the rein again he will be light in your hand. As you are doing this, watch his footfall, see whether his hind legs are stepping short of the fore feet, going into the footfall or over, or maybe he is working on $2\frac{1}{4}$ or $2\frac{1}{2}$ tracks with the inside hind either coming into the circle or out towards the outside fore. This usually indicates lack of muscle power in the quarters causing the evasion. Slow work will rectify this with spiral circles 15 to 5 metres. Slow trot on a circle will teach balance and muscle control as well as confidence. Think in terms of your own learning 'comfort zone', would you have been 'thrilled' to be handed the reins of a horse team and told to drive an obstacle in canter on your first lesson? Don't expect your pony to be any different, also don't go to the other extreme and bore him rigid by over repetition of the same item.

Once you have got the feel and consistency required with the long rein lungeing, you can teach collection and lengthening. Then go on to trot through the line of cones (yes, you do have to run!) and get your turns smooth and quick with loops as and when you need them. It is also an ideal way to start teaching obstacle turns with the appropriate verbal commands so that the association begins to form between left and right. Don't get muddled yourself as this will transfer straight to the pony.

Really active and forward trot with nice lateral bend through the cones. Coram's outline is a bit high.

Left hand has come up indicating a shortening of the stride for collected trot and raised poll. Note the swing of the tail and active legs.

Poll too low here for true collection, but quarters active and steps short. A little behind the bit.

Collected trot coming through well.

Super lateral bend working perfectly on two tracks.

Another thing to practise on the long reins is one-handed driving. It is vital that you feel comfortable with this early on in your driving, otherwise it is a big learning step to master later. There are two ways to do this and both are correct. Private Driving and the BDS favour the Coachman Style which has the left rein coming over the top of your left hand between thumb and first finger. The right rein is then placed between second and third fingers and held tightly with third and fourth fingers, while thumb and forefinger are lightly on the left rein. Your right hand holds the whip at an angle of 'ten to ten' from your body and can rest in front of the left hand. There are a variety of ways that the right hand can be used to shorten the reins when necessary.

Top Tip:
Note how the 'driver' is always positioned behind the line of the shoulder – this ensures the pony goes forward into the hand.

Coachman Style.

To turn left you bring your hand back towards your body and twist your wrist up releasing the right rein forward and tightening the left. To go right twist your wrist down, sending your thumb forward, this releases the left rein and tightens the right.

Sports Driving and pleasure driving generally use both hands, one on each rein, as in riding. However, it is imperative that you know how to drive one handed for numerous reasons. The Continental Bridge is often used whereby the reins are taken in the left hand. Turn your left hand palm down, bring your right hand across the back of your left hand and pick up the right rein with the thumb and forefinger of your left hand and grip the rein through the full width of your left hand. By keeping your left hand palm down you can now turn to the right by twisting your wrist and knuckles to the right, or left by twisting them the other way. This movement releases the outside rein and tightens the inside rein which indicates the direction you wish to turn.

TOP LEFT:
Continental Bridge.

TOP RIGHT:
Left Turn – *right rein is released forward as the left is tightened by turning the knuckles to the left.*

Right Turn – *the left rein is released forward as the right is tightened by the knuckles turning to the right.*

The forefinger just aiding to shorten the rein. This is useful if you haven't set up properly or if you are losing grip of the reins.

This method facilitates a kinder and more negotiating feel to the mouth. Time is well spent on the ground getting a feel for what you will then take onto the carriage. Working your pony on the bit with soft hands is very satisfying.

ABOVE LEFT:
Reins needing to be shortened.

ABOVE RIGHT:
Using a 'half bridge' to keep both reins stable while sliding left hand down rein to shorten.

Ridden and Driven Schooling

Riding plays a vital part in the training of your pony to drive. If you are unable to ride, long reining is the next best thing, or find a rider who will work the pony to your specification. Although the pony is pulling a carriage we are still aiming to have the same technically correct criteria as that of the ridden discipline. We want obedience, lightness and active paces working through from behind, remaining supple at all times – not much to ask really!

Transitions are the key to balance and quarters being truly engaged. Ride plenty of these into a soft hand and use half halts to initiate the transition. Progressive transitions to start with are acceptable in order to keep the pony off his forehand.

When using a half halt, make sure that you don't pull the rein and release it back to the original position as this means 'slow and go' to the pony and may not make it clear what you need. Relax the pressure of your hand without giving forward. This will bring your pony to the balance you need and keep him there, your legs must maintain a light holding support without your lower leg gripping too much. It is also good to remember to relax the buttocks – as it is easy to get tense in this area which will hamper the suppleness through the pony's loins.

I will again stress the need to teach the pony in a natural way with a double jointed snaffle. Balancing reins, draw reins or any other fashionable 'training tool' are quick fixes and will never teach a

Top Tip:
'Engaged' means the back legs working actively and under the horse and producing the momentum to go forward; not scuffing his toes!

true and constant contact between 'hand and leg' or 'hand and driver'. It may look fancy for a while and gain you short term improved marks but as you climb the scales of competition the gap in the training will become glaringly obvious. There is no substitute for time and clarity and if you don't have time or patience to spare – go and buy a racing car and get your buzz from that!

Most faults that we are correcting are rider/driver induced, so remember that when the pony 'won't' do what you want, perhaps you are pressurising him too much or not telling him in such a way that he understands. Much of the time we expect our ponies to have the vocabulary and education of a college graduate while we are sitting like a lump of stone, either on him or in the carriage! As mentioned before, communication is 90 per cent body language so we need to learn about conversing through this medium and keeping the 10 per cent verbal plain and simple! Remember to use the pony's name followed by the upward action required and a simple 'whoa' for downward transitions followed by the pace. Soften your voice for slowing down and have crisp clear instructions to go faster! The tone of your voice makes all the difference.

So how can you use body language when you are sitting on top or behind and your pony can't see you? It is through feel; relaxing or tightening muscles and allowing the trunk of your body to mirror the direction you wish to go and letting your shoulders follow the shoulders of your pony. So instead of pulling the rein to turn left, turn the trunk of your body, allowing the left elbow to slide past your hip and the right hand to move forward to 'allow' the turn through the outside rein. Your shoulders and waist actually make the turn with your inside leg maintaining the pace and outside leg supporting the quarters. You must always keep focused on the direction you are going so that your body is continually expressing your intent.

It is all right to check what is happening below you but don't focus on the pony all the time, it is like looking at the bonnet of the car, you won't get very far doing that! Focus on where you want to be, not where you are.

Within your transitions using halt, walk, collected trot and working trot, instil discipline for the halt. Encourage your pony to stand square and still. A large number of ponies hate standing, so practising while ridden is great. When you do halt, remember to totally relax yourself so that the pony picks up on that, if you are tense he will be expecting something other than a halt. It is at this stage we need to insist on all transitions being 'on the bit', as this ensures quarters are active and working. Driven transitions are harder as the outline needs to be on the bit while allowing 'top line' stretch to get the carriage moving. It can take six to twelve months for a riding pony to develop the necessary driving muscle.

Sinbad regaining the harmony with his rider, under the stern look of the driver!

If the rider is finding the pony difficult to soften or the pony is evading and the rider not strong enough in the leg to hold him, then the 'driver' can long rein/lunge to encourage softening and can feel for both. Care must be taken not to catch the rein under the rider's feet and knock them off balance. The rein is between the stirrup and girth. This should only be used for ten to fifteen minutes to establish harmony.

Once the pony understands this phase of his education and you are happy with the result, then repeat the exact same process with your carriage. Start off with walk, incorporating circles, deviations and diagonals to maintain interest while practising your transitions. Then progress onto trot work, using the half halt to maintain rhythm and balance. It is better to focus on a slower trot for a week or so as this builds up the muscle tone more quickly.

The next chapter goes into detail on how to school for the requirements of dressage and cones. I will also cover common recurring challenges in Chapter 7 and give some ideas about sorting them out.

Monkland Flyer looking
fresh for the cones phase at
Hopetoun House event. A
well balanced turnout.

5 Dressage and Cones

Dressage

The term 'dressage' puts fear into grown men! One wonders why as the definition of dressage is: 'the training of a horse in obedience and deportment', and it is intended to demonstrate that the driver has the skill and understanding to make something of his pony. Perhaps this will put it into perspective for you. If we can equate it to the start of the speedier sections of Sports Driving, then it may begin to have more appeal. Without the basics in place, no obstacle will be easy to drive. Our ability to be accurate and smooth in the dressage phase has a direct bearing on the cones and marathon results.

So what are we actually looking for?
➤ Freedom and regularity of paces
➤ Harmony
➤ Impulsion
➤ Suppleness
➤ Lightness and submission
➤ Ease of movement
➤ Correct positioning on the move

Probably the best benchmark we can have to gauge the level of the driver and pony is to perform a few transitions from halt through to trot and back down. Balance comes from these. A pony may well trot around an arena in a smooth and regular pace, but when asked to change pace can either throw his head up in the air or pull forward taking the driver off balance too. From this we can deduce that there is no engagement of the quarters to balance the pony and that the hands are likely to be 'demanding' a change as opposed to setting up and then asking. It's at this stage that we need to use 'half halts' so the pony has an idea as to what is expected.

> **Top Tip:**
> Half halts: aren't half way to halting! They are a brilliant aid for rebalancing your pony and maintaining smoothness of pace, even when the pony may have other ideas. We have already referred to squeezing the rein to tighten the contact without a vast movement in the hand. This needs to be refined to get the half halt to make the back end of the pony work harder. As the little finger closes to get the 'big drip' out of the sponge, then without easing the rein at all, the last three fingers squeeze the last 'little drip' out of the sponge and the hand relaxes downwards – not forwards as you do not want to indicate an increase of speed. You are looking for balance and rhythm within the framework of the half halt.

Properly executed, a half halt will soften the mouth as well as achieve balance. So often on a turn off the side of the arena a pony is taken by surprise and will throw his head in the air on the turn. Setting him up with a half halt with the outside rein before the turn will soften the feel of the bit and he will be in balance to make the turn.

Progressive transitions are really good as it takes the 'demand' out of the equation and gives the pony and driver time to practise half halt and softening the reins to allow the pony thinking time from the vocal command. As you become a partnership, the time it takes to come through the transitions reduces until it happens at the letter in the dressage arena.

We need to work on lots of different items so as not to bore the driver and pony. Practise one thing, then take the pressure off and move on to something different. Trot is the dominating pace – collected, working and lengthening/extended. We need to be sure what we are looking for before tackling this task.

Collected trot
This is a shortening of stride and body outline, bringing the poll and crest up much higher than the withers. The speed may be slightly slower than working trot but only marginally, but the rhythm must be

Prince in a long outline, poking nose, no back end engagement, worth about three or four marks in a dressage test, at most! This is also an excellent example of the driver not fitting the carriage properly and the turnout looking wrong.

Prince totally different! Energy producing action and engagement; accepting the contact and listening well to the driver's requests. Note the higher crest and rump.

the same. Imagine someone has got a piece of string to the poll and top of the rump and is pulling them upwards, leaving the pony very active and energised behind, but only able to do short strides. The hind feet must not step into the footfall of the fore feet, but there is still plenty of impulsion.

Working trot

This is a longer outline, still with the pony on the bit but the hind legs 'tracking up' to the fore feet. 'Tracking up' meaning the hind feet land where the front feet have been, encouraging more activity from the quarters. If we allow the pony to 'slop' along in a long outline and above the bit, he is likely to wear out his hind shoes quite quickly and will find the carriage a bit of a burden, as he is not 'getting his hocks under him'. This is what generates the 'push' and energy to build the muscles that make his driving easier.

Working trot.

The distance covered in each stride is very noticeable. As is the lower quarters enabling the thrust from the back end.

Extended/Lengthening

The purpose is to cover more ground through greater impulsion from the quarters, allowing the leg action to get longer. It is not through speed that we get lengthening as that can often come into the category of 'running' across the arena.

Let's work through points that we need in order to satisfy the requirements of a dressage test and the expectations of the judges.

Top Tip:
Remembering how influential our bodies are, we must emulate the shape our pony does in his various trots with our hands. It is similar to a triangle.

collect

lengthen

working

In collection our hands emulate the higher outline (not our shoulders as well though!). Working trot is just balanced and comfortable. Lengthened strides allow the extra engagement from behind and the longer outline, therefore our hands and elbows move forward with the movement. We need to start the lengthening from a few strides of collected.

Freedom and regularity of paces

These can go together as they form part of the essential foundation of the training. The pony needs to go forward free of tension and resistance with regular footfall.

Harmony

Ideally the driver and pony working together with an understanding of each other. In other words, the driver is not to show exasperation or frustration.

Impulsion

This must not be mixed up with speed. It is a desire to go forward willingly with a supple back, enabling the engagement of the quarters, producing a springiness of steps.

Suppleness

The ability of the pony to make the required movements without tension in the outline, lateral bending through the corners and circles.

Lightness and submission

This indicates that training is correct. The back muscles are relaxed with a freely maintained head position; the nose approaching the vertical. The pony is attentive to his job without losing sparkle or becoming irritated.

Ease of movement

This follows on well from lightness and submission as agitation and resistance, either physical or mental, will prevent the 'flow' of what we need to achieve. Unless your pony is relaxed you are unable to use the aids subtly and tactfully, losing the smoothness and 'swing' of the movement.

Correct positioning on the move

Straightness is the key thing here, especially going up the centre line towards a judge. No pony is born with the ability to 'go straight'. We have to develop that through proper training and respect that they all have a 'soft side' and a 'hard side' and we need to develop elasticity and strength in the muscles in order to improve this. Balance and impulsion will be the key factors to driving straight in the same way that lateral flexion will develop for the circles and corners. We are looking for the hind legs to follow and step into the footfall of the fore legs and the pony to be working on two tracks.

Bend

Vital to everything we do and can be the hardest to achieve. We

---

Top Tip:
The Scales of Training

Rhythm

Suppleness

Contact

Impulsion

Straightness

Collection

This first originated in Germany in 1912 and has become the mantra for all dressage enthusiasts.

expect our ponies to bend sideways like a banana, but in actual fact the backbone is unable to move in this way. So it's the stretching and contracting of the muscular system that achieves this.

Halt

Ideally we want to achieve an 'upward transition' to halt with the back end actively engaged and the poll remaining at the same height as in walk, with softness through the jaw. The pony needs to remain straight and motionless.

The rein back

A two-time pace and is only really achievable when the pony has learnt to work in a relaxed and soft outline. Harmonious integration between head, neck, shoulders and hindquarters will then result in a backward movement with no evasion. Sounds so easy when written, not quite the same in practice!

Top Tip:
At the halt the pony must

➢ Stand attentive
➢ Motionless (!)
➢ Straight

A nice square halt although I would like him to be more relaxed in the jaw and on the bit.

Prince showing no resistance into rein back with legs moving as required on the diagonal.

Top Tip:
The rein back must:

➢ Be straight
➢ With no resistance
➢ With legs working in diagonal pairs

Now that we have established the guidelines needed for the dressage, let's go through how to achieve it. Hopefully the lungeing practice has given you an idea of the feel needed in the reins, and watching your pony has given you an idea of what he looks like when you ask a question. That 'feel' now has to go with you to the 'box seat'. I say 'feel' as the view is totally different from the carriage and it is not always clear what you are getting.

The **walk** can be developed on the road as well as in your schooling area. We need energy, rhythm, contact but calm and regular steps. The pony needs to work on the bit and be light in the hand. If the pony is too fast he will lose the four-time beat and become unbalanced. If the outline is too long and low there will not be enough energy from the quarters.

The transition up to **trot** has to be smooth and energised without 'jumping' into it or the pony coming above the bit. In order to set this up, a half halt to engage the quarters and gain the energy and pull needed to take the carriage onwards is useful. At the same time lightly increased contact will indicate your intentions to the horse along with the vocal command. Be careful that as the pony lengthens

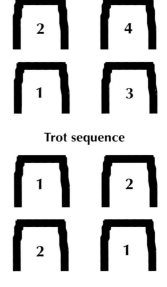

Walk sequence

Trot sequence

In working trot one should be able to draw an imaginary straight line from the bit to the pony's hip. Take a picture and check it out as this will help you to know if you are getting the correct outline.

his top line and engages you don't remain still in your hand, as this could be misunderstood as a reduction in pace. Keep your fingers light and asking to relay the energy from you to the pony, and implying freedom forward into the contact. If your pony doesn't respond to the energy in your voice and hand lightly flick the whip onto the shaft and that should send him on. Plenty of transitions between walk and trot will increase his suppleness and improve engagement. Do remember your half halts each time, as this brings the pony's weight back into the quarters and produces the uphill transition, thus keeping the pony balanced and off his forehand and your reins. Quite quickly they associate the command and half halt and often after practice the voice is sufficient.

It is important to free your arm from the shoulder and follow the movement of the neck during transitions. With the weight of a carriage the pony will be a little longer in his body in order to pull the vehicle than if you were riding. Do not mistake this lengthening for the need to be off the bit. Once we have developed a nice smooth and regular pace we can think about lengthening the trot. We must bear in mind 'lengthen' – this term means everything. Mainly the hind legs *must* come further under the body and forward of the fore legs. Flashy front legs have little to do with technically correct lengthened or extended strides. To set this up we must actively bring the pony's weight back into his quarters through a half

Monkland Flyer extending well and relaxed throughout his outline although not on the bit in the cones. Note how direct the contact is to the bit.

> **Top Tip:**
> Cadence is the quality of trot and canter, elasticity of the pace and the momentary suspension between strides.

halt and then send him forward into a yielding hand that allows the top line to lengthen as the quarters project the hind legs forward, but at the same time maintaining the tempo of the trot. Do not expect too many strides to start with and do make sure you actively end the request for lengthen. So often one sees a competitor 'dribbling' into working trot after the diagonal of lengthen. Don't be one of those!

As your pony is lengthening, keep an even contact to his mouth and match his strides with opposite pulsing of the hands as if you were riding and squeezing with alternate legs to send the hind leg further forward. To get the feel of what you want, trot your pony uphill, they often lengthen and you will feel the moment of 'cadence' between strides. Without this cadence in the extended gaits, the pony will not be truly balanced and capable of executing the movement. Also keep an eye on his bottom, as this is the early indicator of him losing his balance. The 'swing' becomes uneven and he will break pace or hop in his stride. As soon as you see a change in the rhythm, half halt and that should put him back on track.

I think **collection** is quite hard for a novice driver or pony as it takes a lot of muscle strength and control to be correct and is difficult to gauge. The neck needs to be raised for the shoulder to be free and the hocks need to engage to a greater degree, allowing the steps to be short but more active. The tempo is the same as working trot. We need to set up with a half halt into increased contact but more active squeezing of the rein. This restricts a faster pace but energises and elevates the limbs into activity. Raising the hands as well encourages the poll to rise as we shorten the torso. It is imperative that we do not lose regularity and tempo and end up going very slowly. Pulsing of the rein will keep the contact fresh and interesting.

> **Top Tip:**
> Contact = energised response.
> Remember that racehorses race in snaffles – the firmer and more direct the 'feel' the faster they go. Reduced contact and they slow down. If a highly-strung thoroughbred understands that message, we should be able to emulate that for our ponies!

Merlion going forward into collected trot. As his crest raises so do the driver's hands to maintain the direct line of contact.

To get a good **halt** the pony needs to be soft in your hand and balanced through his quarters. Set him up with a half halt, give the vocal command and squeeze the reins again, making sure you are relaxed too. He is to remain as still as possible before moving off. Keep an even contact and a very light squeeze so he doesn't try to lean on your hand. You also need to be ready in case he moves off before you want him to. If your pony is a bit fractious, don't demand he stands for thirty seconds if that is going to wind him up. Ask for a little, praise when you get it and build it up from there.

Rein back needs to be taught from the ground first – in the stable, leading through gates and on the lunge are all ideal places. Say the word 'back' and push his chest gently with a little pressure on the head collar or reins to indicate your intentions. Don't say his name, or 'click' as this is a signal for forward movement and will confuse him. They can't go back and forward at the same time – allegedly! If your pony is slow to cotton on, tap his knees as you say the word 'back' and he will lift his legs back away from the tapping.

On the carriage try your first rein back on an upward slope as this gravity will help and make the movement easier for him. From halt, raise your hand a tiny bit and pulse your reins as you restrict the forward movement and repeat the 'back' word several times. If your pony is not sure, put your groom down and get them to push the chest as you repeat the command. Don't set yourself against him if it is not as flowing as you want. Give him time to think and build up from one diagonal step to the next. We need the rein back to be two-time not four-time!

When practising your flat work don't repeat the same thing for too long as this causes boredom and sets up evasions. A little bit that feels good is more constructive. Putting a test together is not an issue providing you have the basics in place. These being your rhythm, balance, contact and impulsion. Transitions and half halts are the key to smoothness. Every time you turn off the straight side of the arena, half halt with your outside rein, this will help enormously. As you and your pony increase in confidence and strength, this won't be quite so necessary.

Top Tip:
If you can remember to focus forward, look for the turns and reflect the direction through your body, it will be much easier.

Top Tip:
Your pony's nose is taken as the point of accuracy. So you need to stop with his nose on X (not literally!) and no further than his forefeet.

Top Tip:
Indoor dressage always starts in walk, due to lack of space.

(1) Approaching H for a diagonal, half halt.

Positioning in the dressage arena is crucial. If you are accurate, that will help your marks. Some ponies will never be good at dressage, but will make up for it in the cones and marathon. Many of the Junior drivers whom we have started in the sport, have poor dressage marks because they drive my stunt ponies who have a 'day job' in my display, which does not require them to work on the bit or be calm. But they consistently do well in cones and obstacles as they have trained hard on accuracy and smoothness – all of which derives from good grounding.

When you enter the dressage arena to trot to X, don't come in from 20 metres outside the arena as you will start to wobble before you get to X! Enter the arena off a circle with a positive working trot and look for the X marker. Don't be tentative as you get near it, remember your half halts and halt, salute with a big smile, even if you are feeling sick! At least it's refreshing for the judges who have to look at po-faced people for hours on end.

As you get towards C don't turn off 8 metres before it, get as close to the letter as is feasible to get a smooth turn and get yourself on the track well before the corner. Maintain your outside rein contact in case the pony anticipates or is looking at the white boards. When you come to do a diagonal wait until the pad on the pony passes the letter before you turn and remember the half halt as you execute the move. This ensures the carriage leaves the track at the letter and looks very accurate. Do pass through X then focus a metre before the letter you are heading for. This allows the pony to get to the track and turn with the carriage on the track at the letter.

Above:
(2) Merlion has started the turn, the carriage wheel is at H, the driver is looking for the next marker.

Left:
(3) The letter H is out of sight as we are in the middle of the letter thanks to the accurate turn.

(4) Really straight, heading for X.

A really awful corner away from the boards, although the pony has super bend.

Ideal positioning but not always easy to maintain. 'Use of the arena' is a frequently used term and if you miss the boards and corners by 2 metres or so, the judge can hardly commend you on that! Ideally the wheels of the carriage should be 6 to 8 inches off the boards, apart from the corners.

Good corner, close to boards, nice bend and rhythm maintained throughout.

The serpentine is just three or five half 20 metre circles with straight lines in between. The rhythm and tempo are crucial here, so half halts at the start of every bend will set the pony onto his hocks and the half circles will remain smooth. If you are performing a three-loop serpentine, the line is a slight diagonal between the half circles. A five-loop has straight lines between the half circles. Remember to change the bend of the pony as you cross the centre line and set your sights on where you are going, well ahead of arriving there! Do talk to your pony, you have during all your training and it is reassuring for both of you.

For **deviations** make sure you focus on the end of the arena in order to get the correct depth. Ten metres is a quarter of the outdoor arena, half way between the centre line and the side. As you come round to start the deviation, don't leave the side until the pad is at the letter (same as diagonal) and don't be in a hurry to get to the 10 metres. It needs to be a slow shape and as the pony's nose gets to the middle letter, start your return, but again not too quickly; land at the track a metre from the letter.

One handed circles seem to cause angst in most drivers but the more tense you are, the worse they'll be. If your circle is at A or C then sort out your reins, whether coachman or continental, as you

Ollie executing a good one-handed circle. Note the whip held out to side.

come out of the corner, keeping the right hand available for last minute adjustments. The right hand should be held out straight with the whip vertical. It is permissible to use the whip if necessary. During the set up, the inside rein should have been placed shorter than the outside in order to get the turn and shape of the circle. Often through nerves we can lose the rein and not get the turn we need. At this point remember we can move our hands and arm in the opposite direction to the turn to get pressure on the inside rein. You must turn your hand as well so as to release the outside rein or else nothing will happen. A 30 metre circle is 5 metres off the sides so don't slide back to the track until you get to the short side, and near to C or A.

A one handed circle to the right. The ponies are working well together but resistance in the jaw of the nearside pony is affecting the lateral bend. Neither pony is working on the bit – often the case in the early days of training. Otherwise there is plenty to be pleased about. Don't let one or two points that need improving detract from the four or five things that are super.

At the end of the test make sure you ask for a couple of half halts as you power up the centre line to stop at G. It is usually such a relief to have got that far that the halt tends to go out the window. Salute and smile again, a wry one if it's not gone well, and a beamer if it has! If there are judges at E or B salute on the move to them as well as you leave the arena through X. The steward at A also needs a verbal thank you.

Let the experience be a very positive one and use the judges' marks and comments to help with your training. It is great when the range of marks is used and this is helpful to determine the areas that need more practice.

Dressage Scoring System

Points will be awarded for each numbered movement and for each heading under the General Impression, on the following basis:

10	Excellent	5	Sufficient
9	Very good	4	Insufficient
8	Good	3	Fairly bad
7	Fairly good	2	Bad
6	Satisfactory	1	Very bad
0	Not executed		

There is a diagram of the basic dressage movements at Appendix 1.

Cones

These can be frustrating or fascinating or both! The idea of this phase is to test the skill and accuracy of the turnout and also for you to be able to judge pace over distance.

Monkland Flyer powering on in the cones. A good strong trot makes accuracy much easier.

Club novice and indoor cones tend to be run at 220 metres a minute, which is 13.2 kph. Liken that to the Section E times on your marathon if you drive a pony. 230 mtrs per minute is 13.8 kph and is used at Intermediate National and most club classes. At Open National Level you have to do 240 mtrs per minute at 14.4 kph. The Advanced National level do 250 mtrs per minute at 15 kph which is a fast speed at which to be accurate.

The cones are generally set 20 cm wider than the permitted wheel track. Again, practise at a lesser distance. We do 15 cm and it really does make a difference. At some club events, Pre Novice and Novice classes will run at 30 cm over track width and some early season events can do 25 cm over as a warm up! At National Level it is always 20 cm.

Having talked about the time, don't let it be your focus to start with. It is more important to drive clear cones than focus on where to catch up time. Balls down are so demoralising! In your mind's eye you need to see every cone as part of a circle or route that you would take in the dressage. You don't have a problem going across the arena or circling (I hope!) when there are no cones in the arena, so we must lift that confidence to the cones phase. We need to keep a constant rhythm going to make the drive smooth. Once the pony starts to 'duck and dive' between cones you are in trouble and this happens if he gets unbalanced and the pilot isn't sure of his route. Using a half halt gives the hindquarters engagement producing more 'draught' (pull of the carriage). As you increase momentum this reduces the 'power steering' effect so you can place the pony where you need to. You don't want to be slowing down through the cones or one stride before as that makes your accuracy vulnerable. Set yourself up five or six strides before on the straight approach or just before the swing into the cones if approaching on a circle.

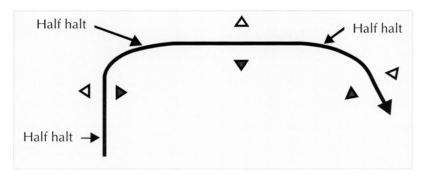

The half halt re-engages the quarters so the pony is not on his forehand and, as you allow the pace to increase, the movement is very positive and direct. On the turn only use your outside hand to half halt, on the straight it is both, but do make sure it's not too strong.

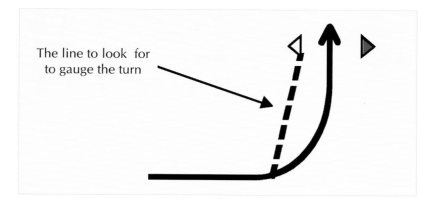

The line to look for
to gauge the turn

A guide as to when to turn into a cone is to judge as the front wheel of a four-wheeler or your knee in a two-wheeler is beginning to come in line with the inside cone of the pair you are aiming for. Then start your turn and this will bring you in line with the pair and keep going straight. Be careful not to turn too quickly after a cone as this can knock them down. Do wait until you are clear of the cone in a two-wheeler, and your groom is clear in a four-wheeler.

It depends how close you are to the cones as to how tight and small the curve of your turn is. It is easier to drive if you are positioned about 7 metres away before you get lined up with your turn in or straight line.

World Gold Medal Winner Ian Bertram competing at Lowther in the cones. Good turning angles from both Ian and the horse.

A tandem driven by Andrew Mylius going through a slalom at Castle Kennedy. Note how the lead pony is close to the outside cone, the wheeler will have plenty of space to get into the middle of the cone.

Zig zag or slalom

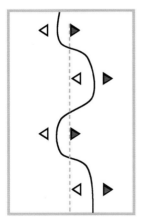

Distance between cones is 10m for pony turnouts; 11m for horse; 12m for horse teams and tandems.

Practise at 2m less, this will then compensate for nerves at the competition!

There is usually only just enough time to get truly straight through the cone.

Driving a zig zag or slalom is always one for holding the breath! We must learn to relax and keep focused on the next cone, not turning too quickly and watching for the inside cone of the turn. You definitely don't want your pony on the forehand for this, or too fast. I tend to encourage a collected trot as both pony and driver learn to negotiate this line. The shorter steps make the turns easier, the pony is already nicely on the contact, listening well and less likely to drop his shoulder on the turn. As the 'feel' of the zig zag becomes more comfortable, then it's time to ask for working trot.

Serpentine

This is another cone combination that's interesting – a row of four cones in a line with 8m between for ponies and single horses, and 10m for horse teams and tandem. I prefer to take a tight line through this, turning as the front wheel gets level with the cones, but some people will take quite a wide circle through. If you can keep a tight line this is a place where you can catch a little time as the distance travelled is less.

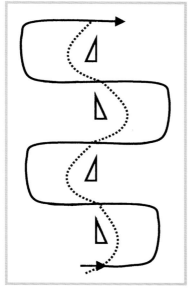

Serpentine showing two different routes through.

ABOVE AND LEFT:
Setting up for a cone on a curve. Merlion is listening well and his hindquarters are really engaged through the cone.

As you practise, both at home and at competitions, the speed will increase as the balance and confidence of the combination grow. Look at the course and see where you can really extend the trot between cones or have to slow to get an awkward angle. Use your half halts to set up for angles and this can help maintain a faster pace with the balance and steering required. Some people canter between cones and if you are travelling the length of the arena this will help your time, but calculate whether it helps you and the pony for the next cones. Personally I feel that a canter lightens the steering of the vehicle and as you come back to a trot before the cone it can be a bit wavering in direction. (Unlike scurry where the ponies are flat out and the vehicle is always in draught. Don't be tempted to drive like that as it is seriously frowned upon and not the point of this exercise.) Nothing can substitute a good extended trot for distances and a working trot for the more accurate turns.

Ann Gilbert with a good strong trot, with her pair perfectly in step. Not sure what's caught her husband's eye though!

Competition cones are very expensive to buy so always a good present idea! Whilst you build your collection, road cones or buckets are a good substitute, but always respect the fact that if you drive over them they can get caught under the carriage and give your pony a fright, or at worse tip you up. Please don't be on your own when practising; even the most reliable pony can drop his shoulder on a turn and the carriage can 'ride' up the cone. (I learned the hard way many years ago when practising bending with road cones for my display. The pony turned too quickly, the two-wheeler went up the cones, over I went and as I fell out I broke my ankle. I had to right

Walking the cones just before your class requires you to be 'dressed'. That means in your attire appropriate for that phase. You can walk prior to the start of the phase in casual dress. Note how the apron is tucked into the waistband out of the way.

Top Tip:
Your groom is not allowed to walk the cones course. Penalties are given if the groom appears to be balancing the carriage in any way as you negotiate the arena. They must sit motionless as they did during the dressage phase.

the carriage on my own and drive back to the yard, a painful lesson never repeated!)

The penalties for knocking a ball off are 3 (5 for indoors). Time is calculated at half a penalty for each second over the time allowed.

Finally walk the course a couple of times to acknowledge the angles and distances, then stand at the start line (out of the way of other competitors!) and go through the course. I am quite sure aliens have a field day watching us carriage drivers making patterns in the air with our fingers as we go through cones and obstacle routes. It is very easy to over walk and get in quite a stew about it. If you have practised enough previously, you know you can do it. So focus forward to where you need to be and your pony will go there.

Top Tip:
At National Level cones courses often include a wooden 'bridge' of some kind (these can also appear in obstacles). If you can, create something at home for your pony to trot over and get accustomed to – even if it is only a sheet of chipboard secured to the ground. This will make sure that he doesn't get a fright at the sight and sound of a strange wooden construction.

TOP: *Monkland Flyer coming off the bridge at an angle and collecting for the next cone.*
ABOVE: *The driver focusing on the next cones as she goes through the current one. No point in looking to see if you hit as it's too late and jeopardises your line into the next one!*

Faith Szczuka's team in cones, the driver looking for the next cone and driving the appropriate size of circle to get there.

The author competing at Dalmeny in Scotland.

6 Marathon

The marathon phase of Sports Driving is the most exhilarating part of the competition. One of the delightful things about the sport is that we are privileged to see some of the most beautiful parts of the British countryside during the sections of the marathon, often over private land specially opened up for the event. It also gives you time to relax (in moderation!) into a rhythm, enjoy the ponies and chat things through with your backstepper.

So what exactly is involved? At Club level there are three sections to a marathon; at National level it is usually five sections, but as the requirement for International level competitions is for only three, it does vary. In the final Section E there are obstacles to negotiate. These comprise up to six at Club level and eight at National level. The object is to complete the distance with no overall time faults and a good clean round through the various obstacles each of which are timed. Hopefully with your pony finishing happy and with some 'fuel in the tank'. In order for this objective to be achieved, there has to be a prior investment in time and skill, utilising training, fitness and practice. *(see Chapter 2)*

The most crucial part of a marathon is the obstacle section. This is where a class can be won or lost.

A pair negotiating a particularly colourful and inventive obstacle at Lowther – a giant picnic table and chairs!

Alice Spence at the Junior Championships with Champ.

However, this will only be applicable if your pony arrives at the start of the obstacles section with plenty of energy. So how do we achieve this with no time faults in the early sections and the energy to sprint through the obstacles? The key to this is to train to the speed required in each section according to the size of the animal. For example, a pony of 12hh to 14.2hh needs to trot at 14kph for Section A which can be up to 10km, that breaks down to a maximum of 4.17 minutes per km. Section E is slightly slower at 13kph, which is 4.37 minutes per km. Horses are 15kph for Section A, at 4 minutes per km and 14kph for Section E at 4.17 minutes per km. *(See Speed and Distance charts – Appendices 2 and 3)*

It is vital that you have measured out a kilometre at home and practised your speed with a stopwatch so you know the feel of 13, 14 or 15kph. Do not just train to the maximum time; you will need to be able to come in about 10 to 15 seconds under the maximum for each kilometre in order to have spare time to slow down for rough terrain or heavy going. A smooth, consistent pace will save the muscles much more than if you 'yo-yo' the pace. There is only a two minute window for allowance on the maximum time, so try to cross the line on the middle spot – i.e. if the time for section A is 26 to 28 minutes, come in at 27 minutes which will give you a comfort zone should you need it for whatever reason.

The Walk section can be madly frustrating! So often the end is in sight and you have 30 seconds left to make the distance. Trotting is absolutely out; an unintentional break of pace for a maximum of 5 seconds is permitted. If this happens, try to use the brake on the vehicle to slow the pony back down rather than too much pull on the reins, as this will keep a longer outline and help get back into a swinging walk. The more pull on the rein, the more likely they are to jog as the outline shortens up. Walking uphill on grass at the correct pace is not easy, so do encourage your pony when on exercise into a long, free walk.

This section is usually 1km (maximum 1km, minimum 800 metres) but can vary depending on the event. The time for ponies is 10 minutes for the 1km which is 6kph, or 7kph for horses which equates to 8.34 minutes maximum. Again use your measured distance to practise the times. A good free walk for that distance does need practice. Please don't just use the road to learn your times because most of an event is held on grass and tracks that sap energy much faster than you bargained for. Just because your pony can trot 7 miles on the road with no break does not mean it is fit. Trot around a large field for 5km and then see how he's puffing! By the time you get to the obstacles he will be walking!

After the Walk section there is a compulsory ten minute halt. This is where you need to cool your pony down if he's very sweaty (water is always available) and offer him a small drink. If he won't drink it is quite handy to have some fruit to offer him, either grapes or a few slices of apple as this will get some moisture into him. I do strongly recommend that whilst he is standing you cover his loins with a small lightweight rug. He has worked hard to get you as far as the halt, his muscles are warm and he is then expected to really operate in the last section, so leaving his loins to get cold is asking for trouble. You will never see a racehorse, eventer or show jumper in between phases without a rug. Driving ponies are equally performance orientated so treat them as the athletes they are. I use a fleece most of the year, but if it is very hot, a thin sweat rug, neither of which adds weight to your spares kit. Check too, that there are no harness rubs and all is in order for the next section.

With a five section marathon, the first 10 minute halt is at the end of Section B – the walk section of no more than 1km. Section C is a fast trot of no more than 4 kilometres. The speed for ponies for this is 17kph, horses 19kph, which is a good lengthened trot stride all the way. The window for this section is one minute and it can be a challenge. Following this is another walk section (D) for a similar distance to the first walk and then another ten minute halt before the obstacles in Section E. At Club events small ponies and newcomers are given a speed of 12kph for sections A and E.

The Obstacles

So what is an obstacle? It is a designed construction to be driven as the key element in the last section of a marathon. It can be made up of any kind of material that doesn't pose a danger to the pony or driver. Gaps of not less than 2.5 metres called 'gates' are situated within the obstacle and are lettered to be driven in order.

For example, a cluster of trees can be used to make 'gates', or potato boxes, poles, rails, barrels, walls, hedges, bridges etc, and within the design some are decorated with flags, animal designs, dummies or whatever is in the imagination of the course designer.

Lord Onslow with his team of palominos at Lowther.

BELOW:
The author with a Welsh Cob horse at Hopetoun House.

ABOVE:
Decorated Christmas trees with protective wooden boxes. Fairy wings on the top of the trees indicating the gates.

LEFT:
A maypole with ribbons overhead.

A well decorated and 'full' obstacle means it is easier to lose your way.

A plainer obstacle makes it easier to see the next gate.

When a team has different ideas to the driver! The leaders having a discussion with the driver over the bottoms of the wheelers!

The walking of an obstacle to learn your route through it must never be underestimated. Each one will have a start and finish flag a minimum of 20 metres from the nearest compulsory gate. Each gate will be lettered A to E with a possible F at the discretion of the course builder. Occasionally there will be a 'pick your own route' obstacle where the gates are marked with red on the right and white on the left. You have to decide which order to drive them. With a lettered obstacle the competitor must proceed through them in alphabetical order. Once a gate is driven in the correct sequence then it becomes a 'dead gate' and can be driven either way en route

to another one. Should adrenalin get the better of you, a gate be missed altogether and you have passed over the finish line, then sadly that is elimination. However, if you or your groom realise before leaving the obstacle, go back to the missed gate and re-drive the obstacle from there in the correct sequence you will add 20 penalties to your score along with time faults, but not face elimination.

The same procedure is necessary if you mistakenly drive a gate backwards or in the incorrect order. You must go back to the missed gate and continue in the right order, and again you will earn 20 penalties for a 'corrected course'. Don't be disheartened when this happens (as you might be) but rather profit from the annoyance factor and learn why it happened. Was the route suitable for your pony? Where you going too fast or asking too much? Or were you not concentrating?

Walking an obstacle is essential to show you how to drive it and memorise your route. Firstly check where all the letters are; look at the ground conditions – is it wet or rock hard? Familiarise yourself with the position of all the letters or gates and when you've done that go back to the start flag and locate letter A. As the driver you can suggest to your backstepper that they stand at the gate looking through it in the correct direction, the red letter always on your right and white on the left. This will indicate the route to get to that gate. Watch when walking that you don't go through another letter on your way to A, then at A do the same for B. There will invariably be one or two different routes to get to the letters and as long as you don't go through a gate in the wrong sequence it is acceptable to choose the route you think most suitable.

A few points to remember when deciding which way to go:

➢ Make sure you have checked every option.
➢ Walk all the options to see which feels 'comfortable'.
➢ If undecided, pace the routes and count the number of changes of direction (each change representing the time it takes to walk five paces, approximately).
➢ The shortest route is not always the quickest.
➢ Appreciate your own ability and that of your pony.
➢ Don't forget to walk from the last 'gate' to the finish line.

The obstacle is timed from the moment your pony's nose goes over the start line to when it returns to the finish line. No matter how laid back we try to be, as regards being competitive, once the clock is ticking reason can desert even the most sensible driver. We can end up in a pickle in what seemed the most clear and easy obstacle when we walked it. In order to help prevent this happening we need to be aware of various things.

Sue Denny and her very successful pony who is a wizard at tight routes and keeping it smooth.

Firstly the pony – how many miles on the clock do they have? If they are a 'school master' then they may have the experience to get you out of your pickle, having been there many times before. If the combination is still relatively green, then do please consider taking long and flowing routes. The pace will be much smoother and it will feel good for pony and driver. There is nothing worse than trying to go for the 'quick' short route and ending up pulling the pony round, getting him jammed onto the shaft, and no amount of hauling can get him off the rail or pole. You'll lose all pace and walking round is not the best morale booster. I have won marathons by taking the long routes and keeping up a consistent pace through all the gates and changes of direction. This gives the pony space to see clearly where I'm expecting him to go.

If he is quite light and bouncy in his stride then he is more suited to the quick tight turns; but if he is a little wooden and on the forehand then longer options will appeal more.

Think about his size too, tiny ponies will tire more quickly if you take a long route and a large horse may struggle to get the tight 'pony' routes. Multiples tend to go for the longer option, especially tandems and teams. On the whole, with good judgement, a pony pair will follow the same route as the singles.

Ann Gilbert with her pair, going on at a good pace and setting up for the next turn.

George Bowman is the supreme master with his team. His rein handling is superb and his team is always listening for the next command. A joy to watch!

George Bowman at Lowther. Note how the leaders are through the gap whilst the wheelers are still going forward to clear the carriage of the posts before they can turn.

Once you have the route decided, make a conscious note of the terrain if you haven't already done this when deciding where to drive. It must be a team effort as your backstepper is the key to how fast and smooth you can go. Wet conditions can play havoc with the back end of a four wheel vehicle, making it very unstable on corners and fast exits to the flags. On turns where the course is rutted from previous competitors, if the backstepper is not 'holding down' the inside wheel with all their weight, then the vehicle can flip very easily as the offside wheel digs into the ruts. Going down steep slopes the weight on the back needs to be very low to enhance the use of brakes, in other words – 'bum over the back edge'!

Going down a steep slope, the groom has transferred her position right to the back of the carriage to help the effectiveness of the brakes.

Going along a slope, as opposed to down it, your backstepper's weight should be kept leaning into the hill. Should a turn be on the slope, keep the weight uphill until half way round the turn and then change sides to maintain weight on the uphill side of the carriage. On the straight, keep weight even through both legs, with your legs slightly apart so you are ready for the next turn.

Having noted how and where the backstepper is going to be positioned, as the driver you must be aware of dips, tree roots, posts, water or anything else that may affect the smooth running of the carriage and efficiency of the backstepper. It can take very little for them to lose their balance and fall off! With a two-wheeler at Club events the same awareness applies, sitting 'side by side' makes the vehicle harder to balance and manoeuvre.

ABOVE:
Pat Cooper and her coloured tandem at Lowther negotiating a difficult right turn on the bank. Note how her backstepper is leaning into the hill to balance the carriage as it makes the turn around the post.

LEFT:
All three leaning well into the turn and enjoying the route.

A two-wheeler well positioned with the groom indicating clearly where to go next!

Good position from the backstepper, keeping the weight low.

Ian and Catriona Bertram – a gold medal winning combination. Note the left back wheel digging in, if the back stepper had been on the left, this could have tipped.

At least this team all agree they are turning right!

How do we learn to drive Obstacles?

The only way that smooth obstacle driving will happen is with a thorough understanding of how the pony moves and how to produce good circles and shapes in dressage *(see chapter 5)*. If you look at an obstacle, think of every turn as part of a circle, whether it be a 5 metre circle or 25 metres. If you are making a turn that is V-shaped, then your pony will lose momentum and use a lot more energy slowing and speeding up than a continual line at a constant speed. This applies at any pace, whether it be a trot or fast canter.

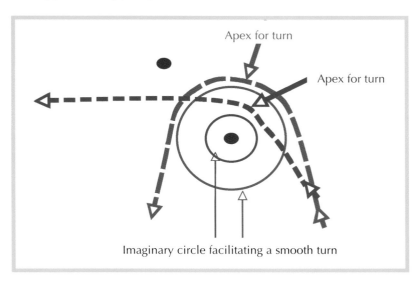

Apex for turn

Apex for turn

Imaginary circle facilitating a smooth turn

Green and blue arrows indicate the point at which the turn changes direction at the apex of the imaginary circle. The apex is at two different positions on the different coloured lines depending on where the pony has to go next.

Take the basis of a serpentine, where there are several changes of direction, but no alteration in smoothness of pace as a starting point. Balancing your pony onto the outside rein is imperative as this controls the size of the turn or circle required, also mirror the turn size with your body which will ensure a smooth manoeuvre that is comfortable for all concerned. If you practise your change of directions through the serpentine and reduce the size of the half circles from 20 metres to 7 metres gradually, you will all become comfortable with the question that is being asked. As you ask for every change of direction use a word to associate with that command. This may be as simple as 'left', 'right', or 'forward', or use the traditional 'come', 'git' and 'forward'. The important thing is to always be clear and don't say 'left' and pull on the 'right' rein!

As we have already said, a really good way to teach your pony to turn on voice commands is to long rein him through a line of cones. Run behind him in trot and weave in and out of the cones using your voice every time you turn, circle around the top cone and then repeat down the line. When looking at a turn make sure you are aware of where the apex of the circle or turn is, if you misjudge your turn in, it will be a frantic sort out as you head for an obstacle gate. The success of the turn doesn't start when you go through the letters; it is set up some distance away.

Boyd Exell, champion team driver showing a good example of taking a loop to get a team round a tight turn. Note how much his body has turned to facilitate the turn and his grooms are focused as well. The belt is only fixed to one side of the carriage and the other end is held by the groom behind. This is a good idea to help keep the driver in place as the power and thrust of a team is enormous.

Good examples of how the angle of the driver influences the turn.

Top Tip:
Remember to focus forward to your destination and don't get stuck looking at the bonnet!

Here the drivers and backsteppers are focused on where they are going next and the ponies mirroring them!

The driver angle perfectly matches that of the pony. Note how the outside rein is balancing the turn.

The backstepper is really balancing the vehicle on the inside of a tight turn and the driver is guiding the pony round with the whip.

LEFT:
The outside rein here has been given to allow the turn into the inside rein.

BELOW:
The outside rein keeping the balance and size of the turn.

Use your imagination to create turns or full circles but focus on clear and precise vocal commands being matched with gentle but quick rein handling. As you and your pony gain confidence, then you will be looking to go faster! When your pony has trust in you regarding route clarity and smooth turns he will take himself up a gear or two. Don't chase on for speed to start with; if you are indecisive your pony may start to lose confidence and 'back off' the obstacle. The canter will come naturally. One of my best ponies would only ever trot the first two gates of the first obstacle to feel his way, then he flew, rarely being beaten in that phase. Whereas my indoor pair likes to have a sprint start from the outset – they are all different, thankfully!

The author's pair powering through an indoor obstacle …

… and with a single pony, powering out of an obstacle! Note how the rein is allowing total freedom to stretch the outline for the impulsion to go forward.

Lovely pace and control at the exit of the obstacle.

Slightly flamboyant reins as the horse pulls up out of the water but this has ensured that he has the opportunity to really stretch on the pull out.

It is a good idea to be up on your times by about 1½ minutes before you get to the first obstacle as this will allow your pony a breather in between each obstacle. Obviously everyone has a system which suits them, but I have found that walking for about 100 metres before the start of each obstacle (after the first one) gives the pony a short breather and takes the pressure off them. Then they can really do a sprint start into the obstacle. A steady trot afterwards winds the muscles down and helps reduce the possibility of strains.

From the last obstacle gate to the exit flags you must still concentrate as it is quite easy to think you have 'finished', easing off the pace and steering – don't!

Relax between obstacles and think of the route for the next one you are going to drive. If your time on the stopwatch is showing that you are early, then do come back to a walk as this does re-energise your pony. It is a big advantage if you can have your obstacles videoed. I have learned much from watching videos and altered both route planning and driving technique accordingly.

From the last obstacle to the finish or 500 metres to finish you must not stop, deviate from the route, or circle in order to lose time, nor may you canter to make up for lateness!

The role of the backstepper

The job of the backstepper or groom is almost as crucial as that of the driver – they hold the key to safe driving. They are there to hold the pony before you set off and attend to incidents along the way. They can be the driver's 'eyes' for hazards if the driver is concentrating on the pony for a variety of reasons – looking out for traffic, plastic bags or other potential issues. Should the harness need attending to, they will dismount from the carriage and sort out the problem while the driver maintains control from the box seat. In the obstacles section of a marathon the driver could not function without their backstepper to keep the balance of the carriage through the turns and on the way out at speed. Do not ever think it is safe to put a completely novice person on the back of a carriage and whizz round a field to give them a thrill. It could end in a tip up and the consequences are ongoing.

Make sure you both have the same terminology for all the equipment and follow the same safety procedures. In outdoor competition the groom must always be seated for the dressage and cones and *must not* speak to the driver.

One of the many roles of a groom is to make sure your driver is also correctly equipped. For the dressage the driver must have brown gloves, apron, whip and hat. Don't forget to put the competitor number either on the vehicle or in a bib on yourself! Do keep your driver's morale up as well! They often get cross with themselves or disappointed, and at the end of the day you should both be having fun!

For the marathon phase both the driver and backstepper are united in one aim – getting through the finishing line safely having had a super drive – most of the time you'll achieve this!

Walk the obstacles, plan your route and take note of any 'compulsory gates' (usually on the route of the marathon to keep you on the measured course). These have markers which are white on the left and red on the right, usually as a pair but sometimes you will just see either a single white or red one. Make sure you pass through all of these (on the correct side if they are single!) otherwise you will be eliminated. You should have picked up all the required information for these and any hazards at the marathon briefing. It is probably a good idea to work out your times for the sections before you go to the beer tent! *(see Marathon times sheets in the Appendices)*

On the day, to take some pressure off your driver, as the backstepper you should be responsible for seeing that the carriage is equipped and ready. Firstly make sure your wheels have been put back to the 125cm width. There must be a full set of spares and straps and you must have a whip. Put a stopwatch on the vehicle as well as one on yourself and the driver. Three may seem a lot but at some time you will be glad of them! Your time sheet and course information is either attached to the vehicle or in the bib on the back of your driver where you can read them easily.

Top Tip:
The spares kit needs to consist of:

➤ Spare rein
➤ Spare trace
➤ Spanner (ensure same size as nuts on the carriage)
➤ Rope
➤ Tape
➤ Cable ties
➤ Multi-purpose penknife
➤ Lightweight rug
➤ Chocolate bar/water or any other refreshment you feel you may need between sections
➤ Grapes (for the pony, not you!)

Once at the start area, check your driver is ok and then go to the official to get your 'green card'. *(There is a copy of one of these at Appendix 4)* This is the record of your times in each section and will be completed by stewards along the way. Keep this safe and dry – the best place is in the front of your number bib. You will be counted down from ten seconds and you must be on the vehicle before it goes through the start flags. Watch for the kilometre markers (on your right) and check your time sheet with the stopwatches to see if you are at the right pace for the section. Discuss with the driver whether you may be too fast or too slow and they can adjust the pace accordingly. You need to control the pace by watching the km markers and the time so that you arrive in the 'middle of the window' of your minimum and maximum times allowed at the end of each section. As you cross the line stop the watches and give your 'green card' to the timekeeper who will write down the time on it.

Appendix 5 has a quick competition reference checklist that you may find useful.

Do take a minute to check if the time on the card matches that on your watches. For example: Your section time allowed was 26 to 28 minutes; your actual start time was 11.10am and the timekeeper at the end of Section A has written down 11.37.05. Do a quick sum and work out that this is 27 minutes and 5 seconds. That's within your time allowed and should match your watches to within a few seconds. Should the time on the card and that on your watches vary significantly you must question it with the timekeeper. It will either be an error easily rectified or, if not, it must be reported at the halt and at the finish in order for the matter to be investigated. Don't wait until the scores are up and wonder why you have time penalties in the sections when you knew your watches and your time sheet matched! Do the checks all through the sections and if you have had any hold-ups or problems tell the official at the end and they will take up the matter and clarify it.

Please remember to thank everyone you encounter who has given up time to facilitate the competition and your pleasure.

7 Problems

In this chapter we are going to look at common problems in schooling and other areas. Ideally we would like to resolve them before they become an issue and then hopefully our 'problems' are just a 'challenge'!

Firstly we need to be aware that we exert 90 per cent of ourselves on our pony and that they can be a reflection of our ability to train them for the job in hand. Human logic is not always the same as the pony's and not necessarily what they need! It is so important to actually stand back and analyse the message or situation that we want to deliver and then ask ourselves 'is this clear enough for the *pony* to understand?' Quite often we are unaware of what message we are actually delivering and yet become intolerant of the response we receive.

One exercise, which I am using more and more, is that of sitting the driver onto a four-wheel carriage with a pair or reins and me on the other end! I then look away from the driver and ask for various paces. I then reverse the task and give back the driver the messages that I received for each transition and command. In every case the drivers have been utterly amazed and had no idea that they were either so harsh in their hands or were giving muddled messages. Many have said: 'No wonder my pony feels so strong. I am not in sympathy with him at all'. It is a very powerful training tool and can be great fun too. 'Feedback' technique is used in interpersonal skills training in the corporate work place and it integrates well into equestrian communication skills.

We can then take this a step further in the way we deal with incidents when the pony is not performing the request or behaving inappropriately. Every living creature is guilty of attention-seeking behaviour, how it is controlled is down to us. If, for instance, your pony paws at the ground when tied up, that is not acceptable. Instinctively we will go to the pony, reprimand him and walk away – only for him to start again. This cycle can continue for a while, often the voice is raised and then possibly he is given a slap on the shoulder. The message you are giving to the pony is that if he does something to get your attention, you will go over, even if he gets shouted at. He is getting what he wants and can see no reason to stop pawing. However if you steadfastly refuse to acknowledge the pony in any way when he is pawing, then go to him the minute he stops and reward him with a pat and fuss, he will associate the last thing he did with the praise – that was standing still.

The key is to ignore bad behaviour and reward good *as it happens*. Your voice is incredibly important, the tone and way you say the word, similar to the vocal commands we have discussed, but an extension of them. Incorrect performance or stroppy attitude is ignored with silence, while correct performance or trying is praised with the voice or hand if riding. The number of ponies that nap or refuse to go forward and continue to do so are almost encouraged to carry on due to our handling of the situation. The more you kick, use the whip and shout, the less cooperation you will get and the more stubborn you both become. Take one person away from the argument and you don't have one! Try sitting there as neutral as possible, no voice, no commands, no expectations but looking up. It may take a little while but the pony will soon move on and as soon as they do, praise them. Every time they stop don't join the argument, be neutral and very quickly the pony will give up as it is no longer any fun to bait the human!

People also often say 'My pony is a lazy so and so and won't go!' How about analysing why? The chances are you have long flappy reins and are looking down. Get your nose out of the 'road map', and look for the signposts then your car would go and so will your pony!

This is not taking a namby pamby wimpy attitude to sorting an issue, it is the opposite, using brainpower and sensitivity. It is the same as dealing with teenagers. Shout and bawl at them and you will have fireworks, go along with them and they'll come round to your way, but let them think it was their idea!

Case study:

Becky, a lovely teenager worked on this theory with her riding horse Angel, who quite frankly had been foul on numerous occasions and really frightened her. The mare was fundamentally gorgeous but her previous history had caused various behavioural problems to become established. As the rider is young her natural instinct and subconscious was allowing the mare to continue with her appalling behaviour. Angel refused to go forward, hack out down the lane, turn a certain way, leave the collecting ring etc. She set her jaw so she couldn't be stopped, throwing all these strops as and when she felt like it.

The key to the mare was to recognise what a nice personality she really had, and that she was not intentionally setting out to be difficult. It was her way of protecting herself from fear and angst. So we stopped all forms of potential disagreement! When the mare refused to go forward in the direction we had asked we sat still, talked among ourselves and said nothing until her muscles relaxed and then turned her away from the disputed direction and off she

Top Tip:
High spirits need to be tolerated and channelled. Disobedience should be dealt with firmly but fairly.

went freely; the turn inducing the forward movement. She was then brought back to the direction she first refused to go in and praised as she continued. No forward leg pressure was used, instead a light holding support, voice and guiding hands. If she 'jammed up' again we repeated the process gradually building up the win-win scenario that is needed in a successful partnership. Over a period of time, each area of antagonism was reduced and the confidence between the two grew.

Both had to work hard and there were setbacks, but each time they were quicker to overcome. Eighteen months after being too scared to ride the mare at home, Becky and Angel competed at a cross-country event and went clear. The achievement was like winning a gold medal! It proves that spending time to understand what the pony is telling us through bad behaviour makes it possible to overcome and the gremlins don't reappear because the pony believes they have won, whereas, in fact, we have facilitated a new way of learning for them, with no pressure. As a codicil to the story of this mare, we have also broken her to drive and she is accepting her new skill well!

Becky with Angel – aptly named! She is getting miles on the clock, note the lunge line attached to the headcollar and going back to the groom, a safeguard in case of a fright.

Most evasions are just a way of telling us that something hurts, is uncomfortable or they just don't understand. Once we tune into the animal's way of communication then we can set about developing our skills to being clearer and simpler. There are those who think there is great mystery to training but actually, the simpler the better and common sense is the main requirement.

Driving straight

Driving a straight line is one of the hardest things, especially from A to G in the arena! Wiggly and crooked halts feature in many tests, so why? Probably the line wiggles because the pony is on his forehand; we forgot the half halt just before the turn onto the centre line and we just can't face looking the judge in the eye, so are focused on the 'bonnet' and have no chance of going anywhere with purpose. The halt will be crooked as the planning went out of the window and your reins will not have been even in their request to halt. We could also have a 'dive into halt' or a 'died into halt'! This will result from the pony being totally on the forehand and too fast into halt. Work on your half halts to bring the quarters more actively under the pony and go back to thinking of an 'uphill' transition as opposed to 'thank goodness we didn't hit the judge's car'! It is easy to forget to be soft in the hand as we ask for transitions and by just having a constant pull it produces a negative result.

Merlion driving very straight along the side. The author is actually asking for poll flexion to the left to keep the line. Her left hand has come across in line with his wither and the right hand has allowed the rein.

The halt

If the halt is inattentive this can be for a number of reasons – a volatile pony, distractions, nerves from the driver, novice pony and not enough training are at the top of the list. Try not to be in a rush, a deep breath can help both of you and keep your reins with a bit of life in them, rather than taut and resisting. A calm command is more effective than a desperate shout to 'stand' or even using the whip. Insist on at least three seconds (seems like a lifetime when they are messing around!) of halt and then as you ask them on, make sure you give enough in the hand as they take up the slack on the traces. There is nothing worse than for them to either 'smack' into the collar or reins – an unpleasant habit.

Not the best halt that Prince is capable of and his driver is looking anxious as she tries to correct it.

A consideration

If you are standing in a line at the cashpoint and the person behind is quite close and looking at you, the feeling you get is that of burning discomfort and you want to step away to create the 'personal space' that you feel is acceptable. This is non verbal or physical communication, but is very real and powerful. Consider this when you are staring intently at your pony when schooling and trying to get something right. Give him a break – look up and away from him and I bet what you are working on will improve!

A far better, attentive halt from the combination this time!

A consideration
Getting agitated in the halt and raising your voice is like shouting at a child to go to sleep … won't work long term!

It is imperative that you work on a safe and relaxed halt as so many of your driving phases both in competition and in general depend on the pony standing patiently. Should your pony take matters into his own hooves and start to rear then you must not present him at another competition until this is sorted. Utilise a person on the ground as you come to halt. Let the pony see the person and if necessary clip a rope onto the headcollar to help hold him still (better than constant pull on the reins). Gentle soothing from the handler will distract the pony from the 'issue' of standing. Be satisfied with a few seconds to start with and ask for walk on. Build this up to the ten seconds you need in the dressage and beyond as if at a road junction. Gradually move your helper out of the line of vision but near enough to be helpful if needed. Quite soon the pony will have built his confidence and be able to chill out at the halt, only don't go the other way and let him rest a leg during the test!

The rein back

Rearing in the rein back is another uncomfortable experience. This can be a result of genuine back pain or a mixed message from the driver. How many times are you guilty of saying 'back' and then clicking? As the pony moves forward in response to the 'click', which he understands to be forward, you slam on the brake and pull at his mouth harder. This has now totally scrambled his brain causing him to go the only way left which is UP. It serves you right if it gave you a fright – DON'T CONFUSE YOUR PONY! Go back to the explanation of how to achieve a harmonious rein back in Chapter 5. Do also check the pony's teeth and back as these can have an influence if there is discomfort.

Barney has gone deaf to rein back!

Ooops – TomTom saying 'No' to rein back! A totally disunited pair!

The offside pony has decided to lean off the pole so the grey pony is matching the angle. Even the legs go in at the angle as more pressure is put on the pole and outside shoulders.

Leaning on your hand

Probably the most frequent issue is the pony being heavy in transitions, leaning on your hand and getting gradually stronger. Well sadly it will be all your doing or that of the previous owner. Why? Because you are giving him something to pull against. By now I hope you are aware of my aversion to 'strong bits' as they prevent negotiation and softness, especially when it's needed. If the pony takes 'a hold' the only way to stop him is to soften and massage your contact and give him a chance to 'back down'. Should matters be so bad that the pony is actually 'bolting', then nothing will stop him. With continued poll pressure, curb pressure, ports and single joints digging in around his jaw, he is hardly going to give in gracefully. It will be through absolute discomfort and pain that he comes back. Is that what you want for your pony?

If your pony is already at this stage, then go back to lungeing and try a double jointed snaffle and flash noseband. It is your technique that has to improve – lead by example. As you feel the pony lean, give one rein totally to him and see what happens. The other rein, usually your outside, must still be on the contact with intermittent pulsing. The pony won't go far, he will not run away but come back to find your hand or go long and low and slow the pace down. Build

A consideration
Pulling or leaning is a two way operation – conscious or not. Look at pairs – when one pony leans onto or off the pole the other one involuntarily does the same to balance the equation until it becomes impossible to continue. Liken this to your hands and the pony's mouth.

back your relationship and then put into practice your observations in the carriage. LESS IS ALWAYS MORE. We are dealing with athletes not delinquents.

Develop your technique of half halts, squeezing the 'sponge' and tweaking the rein in a smooth rhythm to help with all situations. It is your bank of knowledge so use it according to the occasion and what you deem fit.

Balance, tempo and rhythm can only be developed in a harmonious partnership and comfortable work atmosphere. As soon as your pony starts to get strong or lean on you, then open your lower fingers of one hand to free a little rein, then slowly close the fingers to tighten it. Then do the same with the other hand. This should ease the 'weight' on the rein. If this doesn't work, ask for a half halt but make sure your rein position doesn't revert to where you started or else you have confused your pony and needlessly pulled him to slow down, then given back to where he was by letting the hand slide forward. The half halt is to bring him back into the framework of 'self carriage' and hopefully keep it.

A consideration
There are many thousands of ponies being driven in traditional driving bits and going well in them; but could that performance be repeated in a snaffle? If not, then the action of the bit is responsible for the head carriage as opposed to the pony's training developing true outline and self-carriage.

Extended trot

Without self carriage when you come to lengthened/extended strides you will end up being very flat, just speeding up for the distance and have no cadence – the springy step. A slight misconception in the driving world is that if your pony has flashy action in front and can throw his front leg well forward from the shoulder, that's enough to

This pony is working from behind to lengthen but is losing some of the impulsion as she is not listening enough to the driver's hands.

get cool marks for extension. True lengthening comes from the hind legs. It is imperative that the hind foot extends well past the footfall of the foreleg to be absolutely correct. So often a flashy front takes the eye off the behind (especially if you are male!) Your pony would have to be an acrobat in some cases to get his back legs so far forward! That's one of the reasons why it is hard to get good marks with Shetlands and Fell ponies as they have restricted shoulder movements and the eye is not focused enough on the quarters.

This pony has potential to lengthen well but is hollow in his back and not producing the outline that would enable further hind leg engagement.

If your pony tends to run on, make sure you half halt him three strides before the point at which you want to start lengthening and ask for a few steps of collected trot. Once the quarters have come up and he is on the bit, ask for lengthening before letting the reins forward to allow the movement to establish, then pulse alternate reins to match his stride. Half halt before coming back into working trot so he doesn't go onto the forehand. Don't expect miracles and once you have lost cadence do come back to working trot. It will get better with time and practice but as with everything we do, a little is better than nothing! It is part of building the 'scales of training'. You will get a higher mark for a short distance of correct lengthened strides than you will for 'running' the whole distance.

A consideration
Set your parameters according to what your aims are. Have the firmness to maintain them and the fairness to bring your pony to meet them in a way that he understands and likes. It is team work that gets the result and there is no 'i' in team!

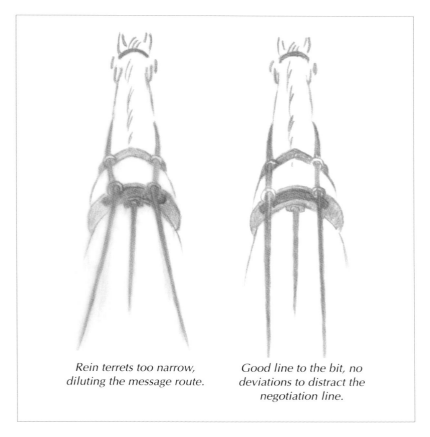

*Rein terrets too narrow,
diluting the message route.*

*Good line to the bit, no
deviations to distract the
negotiation line.*

Top Tip:
If the message you
are delivering is not
getting through
clearly, check the
width of your rein
terrets on the pad.
Sometimes they are
very narrow, which
is fine if you are
doing private
driving, but not
applicable for sports
driving. The line
needs to be as
straight as possible
from his mouth to
your hands.

Circles

Often circles are too small and the wrong shape, followed by the driver complaint of 'he won't stay out' or 'he looks the wrong way'. It is a universal challenge so don't worry too much – it is easily fixed!

Taking the size of the circle first – it is important to walk your dressage test so you can be absolutely sure of where the markers are and how big we need to be. The circle must touch four sides of a square so plan that square and you'll know where you need to come onto the side. Always be looking for the next quarter of the circle from the one you are currently in and it will drive really smoothly and be the right size. Resist the temptation to keep pulling the inside rein for the turn, once the pony's nose is pointing towards the next quarter leave it alone. Use your outside rein to keep the line and your inside just to indicate the direction, not turn. By allowing your shoulders and waist to follow the line of the circle rather than just hands, it will be very smooth and accurate.

If your pony is always looking to the outside on the straight and corners it can be madly frustrating and one is always trying to sort it!

Working on a 20 metre circle, focussing forward to the next quarter of the circle and not asking too much with the inside rein. The ponies should have more lateral bend.

However, we need to check what we are doing first. Remember we are a reflection of them… so if you are on the right rein and the pony is looking to the left, look down at your hands. I bet your left hand is further back than the right, which then means your left shoulder is back and your right one is forward and in actual fact you are 'asking' for a left bend through your body. So the pony is giving what you asked for, even though you didn't consciously want it. You need to alter your body position to reflect more right bend. Shorten your outside rein and take it wider by about 3 inches and slightly forward then squeeze your left fingers to indicate to the pony to move over rather than turn. Don't expect him to move directly over, rather a drift over to the side and keep the head straight. As soon as our hand starts to come towards the centre of your body you are inadvertently setting up a 'block' to the message you want, or you are asking for 'poll flexion' as opposed to lateral bend – and there is a huge difference!

Poll flexion

This is very useful to correct the wrong bend on the straight going into corners and circles. It has to be a moment of correction, as we do want our ponies to work with lateral bend on two tracks. Lateral being the curve (as much as is skeletally possible) from the poll to the dock. The fact that every horse is born with a convex side and a concave side has to be considered in his training and acceptance of his faults. This is why on a circle you will often find the pony pulling out of the circle through his outside shoulder while his head and neck are turned to the inside and it is difficult to get him round. That's very similar to driving cows – the head turns one way and the body continues in another direction!

Quinn our Shorthorn x Galloway driving bovine. This is the second bovine I have successfully taught to ride and drive – and he jumps!

The only time your hand needs to come across your body is to execute poll flexion. It comes in line with the withers and does two or three strong (4 to 5oz) squeezes on the rein to get attention at the same time as your other hand moves forward to allow the flexion that is being asked for by the other rein. If you don't give forwards then the effect of poll flexion is negated as the poll cannot turn and we are unable to straighten the shoulder to bring it back in line with the track and direction we are travelling. For example, we are on the right rein; the pony is looking left on the straight and corners. In order to get the head straight with poll flexion (you have already sorted your body position!), bring your right hand to the centre and squeeze, at the same time move your left hand forward the same amount as your right hand has asked. Then move both hands back to normal position. Repeat several times until the pony understands what is required. Only make the poll flexion request at the start of the corner or circle. The main object is to return to the lateral bend and two-track work.

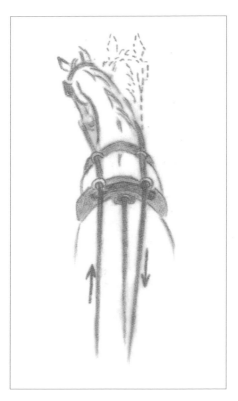

On the right rein when your horse is looking left use poll flexion. Taking the right rein across towards his spine, left hand easing straight forward and the head straightens.

Top Tip:
To get a feel of what the actual weight in your hand is, use old fashioned cooking weights. Start with 8oz – it will surprise you how much that is. Massage it around in your hand and notice how it actually feels lighter when you do that – that's the effect your fingers and moving from the shoulder have on the bars of your pony's mouth. It is no longer a dead weight. Work your way down to 2oz, which is what you are aiming for.

Lateral flexion

To get this lateral flexion this must allow the inside hind leg of the bend freedom to get really under the body and be the driving force of the bend or circle. To do this we must have the rein straight from his mouth, through the wrist, elbow and away past our hip, but don't hold your elbow wide of your body – allow it to hang naturally. If your hand asks towards your tummy then the request stops there and cannot go further. You are unable to increase the request without twisting your wrist at weird angles. If you create this block then your pony will have one too.

Stiffness

Stiffness in paces can often be a result of us not relaxing sufficiently to follow the movement of the pony. If this is not the case, check the pony's back or go back to lungeing and work on spiral circles to soften the muscles that are 'holding'. Collection can show up stiffness in us especially as we try to activate and elevate the pace through the energy in our hands. This can lead to tense buttocks and raised shoulders. Remember to breathe and smile – *both* at the same time and this will free up the energy flow to both you and the pony.

Moving away from flat work to other areas: it is not possible to expand on every possible issue that may happen, I'm just going through the more obvious ones.

Cones

If in the cones your pony starts to drop his shoulder on turns and pops the carriage in to the cones it is likely to be because he is off balance and off the contact. It may also be because you are chasing for the allowed time before he is capable of it, or perhaps you are using your marathon vocabulary for the changes of direction – then you would expect him to drop his shoulder for a quick response. In the first instance use the half halt to regain the hindquarter engagement and bring the pony back onto the contact so he is listening to you and not on his own agenda. We need to get some cadence back into the pace, which will give us the elasticity to then drive him forward. Maintain the tempo rather than flattening him again. Gaining muscular strength and confidence will be more important than speed in the beginning.

Do make a mental note of what you are saying to him. Many people go into 'marathon speak' for the cones phase and that is another way to confuse your pony. We need to drive the cones as we do the dressage – with balance, rhythm and style. Maintain that decorum for this phase and it will be more pleasant for both of you.

Obstacle driving

This is the most exhilarating part of the competition, but things happen quickly as we may only be in the obstacle for 35 to 40 seconds. Well that's the aim anyway!

Going into the obstacle:
Coming through the start gates and your pony's doing a flat trot and fairly deaf to your pleas to go faster!
This may be because:

> - he is actually tired
> - your fitness plan could have been rushed or bypassed
> - he doesn't like obstacles
> - he is uncomfortable with the way he is driven in them
> - you forgot your half halt into collected trot just before the start to energise him and 'spring' him through the gate

United ...

... disunited! Bit of a 'domestic' going on here, the pair haven't sorted out the fact that no one is boss.

In the obstacle:

The next challenge is that as you go towards the obstacle, especially a confusing post and rail one, the pony spends more time weaving than going forward. This is often caused by indecision in the driver and unclear directions to the pony. You need to be categorical where you are going and be looking for the gates well in advance of getting there. Think back to driving a circle, looking into the next quarter whilst driving the current one. Drive towards the A gate and then have B in your sights as you go through A and onwards through the sequence. Your pony will quickly realise you can map read again and pick up on your confidence. Your vocal commands need to be crisp and clear too. You may find some turns tight and the pony is not quick to 'come round'. Positioning through the gate can have an impact. Perhaps during walking you may have forgotten to think of the turn in terms of a circle and misread the size. It may be too ambitious for the level you or your pony are at. It may be a turn for a four-wheeler and you are in a two-wheeler. It may be because you keep pulling for the turn and the pony is unable to give you any more as he is pulled tight on the shaft.

The grey pony already reacting to the body language of the driver and setting up for the right turn.

If this is the case he will evade through his outside shoulder and move diagonally toward that, jamming you onto the rails. The only way out is to leave the inside rein alone and use poll flexion to straighten the pony out and soften the outside shoulder, then progress forward.

Between obstacles:
If you have spare time on the clock I do recommend you give your pony a breather between obstacles. Whether you choose to walk for 100 metres or do a free trot off the contact, it will just give you thinking time for the next obstacle and your pony a moment's 'chill out'.

Monkland Flyer showing no signs of wishing to slow down between obstacles at Alnwick.

The importance of the backstepper

Once you have decided who your backstepper will be, please make sure you train them *(see chapter 8)*. They need to know the appropriate techniques for balancing the carriage on the turns and at speed. Never, once you have both walked the obstacles and decided your route, change your mind without telling your groom. This will cause confusion and the chance of upsetting the balance of the vehicle if they lean in the direction you were planning to go. The following pictures demonstrate how not to do it! There are some excellent views of correct backstepping in chapter 6.

This backstepper is totally inappropriately dressed! No crash hat; tee shirt with no sleeve protection and bra straps showing.
Here she is leaning to the right actively encouraging the inside back wheel to raise, just the thing for a tip-up had we been going faster.

BELOW:
Again on the outside of the turn and 'oh so casual' the way she is holding the carriage

Here she is being totally ineffective. No balance of weight into each leg out towards the wheels. Holding on at the centre of the carriage when her inside hand should be on the inside support of the vehicle. And what's more – she thinks she's going to work for me when she leaves college …?!

8 Competitions

Travelling and stabling your pony

As we become more involved with driving we will be looking towards our first event, what we need for it and how to get everything there. Personal circumstances will dictate a lot and I can only guide you with the options. It is good to look around and ask other competitors, because there are some brilliant ideas out there.

With so much equipment, transport can seem a challenge especially if you are starting on a budget – which is 95 per cent of us! If you are going to a fun day at your local club and you only drive a two-wheeler, you can probably get both pony and dismantled carriage into a trailer, and off you go for the day. For bigger carriages, if you have a pick-up they can be loaded onto that with the pony in a trailer towed behind. That works well for one-day events and indoor competitions – but what if you are away from home for a night? The challenge increases, but carriage drivers are resourceful folk! If you only have the above arrangement, you have to work out where everyone is going to sleep and eat. The easiest way is to have a pen for the pony (electric fencing is not allowed). If he is used to being out at night, then a square of hurdles can be sufficient, providing he can't get his foot stuck through the rails or get over them. These can be fixed to the outside of your trailer for travelling. If you like a cover over the pony then the cheapest way is to have a gazebo awning type tent over the area and pegged down. This is good as it gives shade in the heat and prevents the penned area from turning into a bog in the rain. You can then sleep in the trailer yourself and have a camping stove etc for your sustenance, plus an area in which to sit and stay dry.

There are some amazing trailers on the market that have living at the front with everything you could want and room for a four-wheel carriage, pony and all the equipment you require. You still need to take an enclosure to stable outside. Some trailers have permanent stabling attached, whereby the roof and sides fold out to make the stable and then a hurdle or gate is put on the front.

As you realise what a fabulous sport this is, you may decide to forego the annual holiday or pension fund and save for a wagon with stabling attached. This comes in so many variations that it is impossible to describe them all. My best advice is to go to an event and look at every connotation and decide from there. If you are only

A tidy outfit. The gazebo is for the carriages and the stable is big enough to stall for two but has just the one in it. This does not require an HGV licence if you took your test prior to January 1997

travelling with one pony, you may choose to stable overnight inside the wagon, having taken out the partitions to give him room to turn around and lie down. This does save on the need to scrape up the bedding before leaving the event field. However, a good night's sleep is not always guaranteed as some ponies do rattle around! Once you get two or more ponies, most people stable outside, but it does depend on the size of your wagon.

This is a stabling trailer towed behind a large wagon. A professional outfit and needing an HGV licence.

When thinking about the horse area of any vehicle, make sure it is safe with no rough edges and that there is enough room for him to balance without feeling claustrophobic. There must be a light, which needs to be on when travelling in the dark – it is the law! There must be plenty of air circulating but not a draught. We always travel our ponies in rugs, whatever the weather. The reason behind this is to keep their loins warm as they are standing still, yet using muscles to balance, and are thus vulnerable to temperature changes. You wouldn't find a human athlete travelling to an event in his shorts and tee-shirt whatever the weather. We have spent weeks building up to this so don't jeopardise your performance on the last straight. Do also wrap his legs with some type of boot. Preferably a travelling boot, but some ponies hate them, if so, put on exercise boots instead. Tail bandages or wraps are also a good idea.

When getting organised for the event, I suggest you write a checklist and laminate it so you can tick off the necessities every time you go anywhere. We have learned the hard way over the years and have even managed to turn up at a display with only bridles! The poor girl responsible for loading the wagon nearly died when she realised but luckily we have a large box of spare harness which is always kept in the wagon so we coped.

Here are a few suggestions for your checklist to start you off:

> Passport
> Harness, bridle, bit, reins
> Boots and tape
> Grooming kit
> Spares kit for carriage and general spares
> Rugs: sweat, day rug, stable rug, New Zealand (which can also be used to cover the carriage and keep it dry)
> Feed – supplements and haylage
> Buckets and water
> Bedding
> Muck barrow/bucket/sack and fork
> Carriage and dicky seat
> Lamps (Novice qualifiers and National events)
> Crash hat, apron, whip, gloves, number bib and time sheets
> First aid kit - pony and human
> Generator and petrol if you need it
> Gas
> Sleeping bags and clothes
> Human food
> Pony – there is a tale that an eminent four-in-hand driver arrived at an event without his full team!

You probably won't need all of this just for a one-day event, but you'll be surprised just how much you do require!

> **Top Tip:**
> Legislation on transport changes regularly. Do keep yourself updated and within the law.

Competition procedure – what to expect

Two-day club competition

When you arrive park your vehicle and find either the secretary or stable manager to check that you are parked in a suitable area and to collect your paperwork. This will comprise your number, times for the dressage and marathon, plus any other information relevant to the event. Do READ IT. The dressage comes first, so work your time backwards to how long you need to warm up, then you'll know what time to put to and then harness and groom. Remember, time for a coffee is essential! Also ask your groom to put the wheels out on the carriage as you must be at the correct width for your cones before you start the dressage. Within your timescale you must allow time to walk your cones before your dressage, as they will follow straight after. Should you want to walk the dressage then you need to be there before the start of the competition.

Make sure you know whether you are having a safety check or presentation before your dressage. If you are, present yourself on time, usually 30 minutes before your dressage and do try to relax! The standing inspection is to check fit, safety and cleanliness of the harness and vehicle. The purpose is to inform and be helpful and the judges have heaps of experience to share. However, some can be very intimidating and still think it's part of a BDS showing class, not a club competition! It is very important that you take pride in your turnout every day – not just for this occasion. You need to know how to turn out and polish to a high standard. Do make sure you thoroughly clean your harness both sides and that there is no rust on buckles from sweat. Do not use frayed or worn harness. The dressage and cones phases are the only time you don't use an under headcollar. Polish everything on the carriage including the underside, but not the seats! Brass should be sparkling to within an inch of its life.

The pony must be washed and polished too! Make sure you have cleaned to the roots of both mane and tail – and feathers if he has them. Hooves must be oiled inside and out. Baby oil should be wiped on knees and hocks, through the tail and around the eyes and muzzle. It is incorrect to plait a tail for driving.

For dressage and cones the dress is formal. Lady drivers will wear a smart hat and jacket, with a coordinating apron. Gentlemen drivers wear suits. Backsteppers will usually wear jodhpurs, boots, black jacket, brown gloves, stock or tie and velvet crash hat with a three-phase vehicle. For a single pony/horse in a presentation vehicle the above is acceptable but once you drive at Open National level and with multiples, then the dress tends to be a formal jacket with tails and three buttons at the rear, single breasted with no pocket flaps. This is worn with a top hat and long hair must

Smart turnout of Scottish National Dress.

be secured up in a net or a bun. Brown gloves are a must. It is acceptable to wear national dress, which can look super too! For male backsteppers at Club and lower National classes a suit and bowler looks smart or tweed jacket and bowler. As long as you are smart, clean and 'in keeping with the vehicle' then it will be acceptable.

Jewellery is an emotive issue. Tradition says none; though judges may tolerate it in moderation, and competitors have their personal preferences. It is imperative that you don't have dangly pieces *anywhere* to get caught in equipment. If you wear bracelets hide them up your sleeves or in your gloves. Rings want to be kept small. (I have worn bracelets since I was eighteen, have never taken them off, and don't intend to now. I just keep them under wraps when being judged by those who dislike jewellery.)

Whatever the judge says to you during your standing presentation, thank them and absorb the useful information. Then get on with your warming up for the test ahead.

You must enter the dressage arena within 90 seconds of the signal to start. If there is no steward at A, a horn will sound or car lights flash. Otherwise the steward will wave you in, do say thank you to him.

You may have to resort to some novel ways of getting your groom onto the carriage spotlessly clean!

A brief summary of things to remember about rules but do purchase a rule book from the BHDTA so you can digest all the rules.

Standing presentation for a novice class. Nice tidy turnout though the shafts are a little high as the carriage is sitting slightly back. John Parker is judging, a coachman all his life, he has a wonderful encyclopaedic knowledge and is current Chairman of the British Driving Society.

Entering without a whip, dropping it or putting it down	5 penalties
Competitor entering the arena without jacket/apron/hat/gloves	maximum 5 penalties (unless otherwise stated by the organisers)
Groom without hat or gloves	5 penalties
Entering arena without lamps, rear lights or reflectors (National level)	maximum 5 penalties (lamps are optional at club level)
Error of course	1st time – 5 penalties 2nd time – 10 penalties 3rd time – eliminated
Part of the turnout leaving the arena	marked down for inaccuracy!
All of the turnout leaving the arena	elimination
Use of boots or bandages	10 penalties (but some clubs do allow boots, so check this)

Do remember to remain cheerful and smile whatever happens.

At the cones arena there should be a couple of practice cones to get your eye in and settle the pony into the next job. The stewards here are very helpful and usually allow you another quick walk of the course provided there is time and you respect other competitors. Do make sure your groom is happy to hold your pony (at his head) and that he is settled enough to be safe. Check how the stewards are starting competitors, either by a bell or whistle, or possibly you may start in your own time and the clock starts as you cross the line. Also check whether you are expected to salute the judges before you start. You must start within 60 seconds of the signal otherwise you incur 5 penalties. Also if you 'start' through gates and through the first cones before the official start signal, you get 10 penalties and have to re-start. The start and finish line is neutralised during the course so you can go through it en route to a cone without penalties until the last cone gate. The only time your groom can talk to you is to say that the bell or whistle has rung. If this happens whilst on the course you must stop immediately and see what the jury wants – maybe you have an error of course? You must carry a whip or incur 5 penalties. If you knock a ball off or dislodge any part of a cone you will incur 3 penalties. If you pass through a cone the wrong way or in the incorrect sequence then you get eliminated and you never do it again! Having completed the course thank the judge and wait for your axle width to be measured when you have left the arena.

At a Club two-day event, after your cones phase, you are free to walk the obstacles and socialise. One of the pleasures is chatting to like minded people and having fun, listening to their anecdotes and boy, there'll be some tales! Do remember to attend the marathon briefing in the evening, often held by the secretary's tent or the stable manager's caravan. Attending this is a must. It is here that the course is explained to you and you are told about anything you may need to look out for along the route – low branches, rough tracks etc. Make sure you know what colour the directional arrows will be for your class. This can really cause lots of confusion if there are two courses marked out. You will be told how many compulsory gates there are in each section and you should make a note of these so you can count them off as you go along. You can also ask the officials questions at the briefing, if you are uncertain about anything.

On the morning of the marathon, be up early to walk the obstacles again and feed your pony a minimum of three hours before your start time. Your backstepper is responsible for getting the vehicle sorted and you need to concentrate on the pony. A useful tip once the boots are on is to tape the straps with electrician's tape; this helps to keep them secure. Go round at least twice and fold the end under to make a small tab, otherwise it is really difficult to find the end when you're finished and covered in mud. Tape buckles and ends of straps so they don't flap and remember the tab for easy removal. You may also like to vetwrap the bars of the carriage where the backstepper is most likely to grab hold during the obstacles. This improves grip especially in wet conditions.

Vetwrap used to help increase grip for the back stepper.

Do also tape the buckle on your reins at the bit end. They can inexplicably come undone and this is seriously dangerous. On one notorious occasion at the end of our display, I was on the final lap after the fire stunts when my left rein came off the bit. Luckily, I always go anti-clockwise and the collecting ring was straight ahead, so I galloped full tilt towards the waiting girl grooms who caught us! We never drive anything at speed now without reins taped!

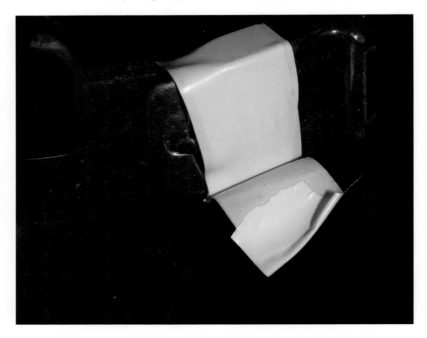

Showing rein buckle taped with tab for quick removal.

Casual, comfortable attire is the order of the day for the marathon with your 'colours' on your tops and the boots on your pony. Personally I feel that jeans are too sloppy, but that's just my preference. I always think one should make an effort to be smart, after all we turn out ponies out to a high standard, so why not ourselves – even if we are all likely to come back covered in mud. Finally, don't forget your number bib, stop watches etc.

At the end of the marathon, take your pony back to the wagon as soon as possible. Take him out of the carriage and throw a rug over his quarters. Then unharness, unboot, wash him down thoroughly and re-rug. Either return him to his stable or let him wander in hand and graze a little once his respiratory system has returned to normal. You must limit his water intake for the first 15 minutes and it is a really good idea to add electrolytes to the water to help re-hydrate him after his efforts.

After all the competitors have completed the course, the scores will be posted as soon as possible. If you have any queries you have

ABOVE:
Cheerful marathon colours!

LEFT:
My early horse pair with the grooms all working hard!

half an hour after they are posted to raise these before the scores are taken to be accepted by competitors. Then the prize giving will follow. Please thank the organisers afterwards, they and their team will have been working hard for days before you arrived and will be there long after you are heading homewards, removing obstacles and restoring the ground. Finally, do take your rubbish home and make sure any bedding or manure is placed in the trailer provided, or on the piles indicated.

A brief summary of some of the rules for the marathon.
(Again, I reiterate – read the rule book, then there are no excuses!)

Vehicle below weight	elimination
Failing to pass through compulsory turning flags in correct sequence	elimination
Each deviation from the course after the last obstacle	10 penalties
Incorrect paces	for every 5 seconds – 1 penalty
Intentional break of pace in walk	elimination
Finishing section E with less horses than required? *(Yes, this is in the rule book!)*	elimination
Finishing section E with a missing wheel *(yes this is in the rules too, see story that follows)*	elimination
Finishing section E with disconnected or missing trace or pole strap	elimination
Failing to pass through entry or exit flags of an obstacle	elimination
Going through a gate in the obstacle in the wrong sequence	elimination
Correcting error of course before leaving obstacle	20 penalties
Grooms dismounting or falling off	10 penalties each time
Driver falling or getting off	20 penalties
Carriage tip up in an obstacle	60 penalties
Exceeding time limit of 5 minutes in an obstacle	elimination
Knock down	2 penalties
Time in obstacle	0.2 penalties per second

When driving began as an FEI discipline in 1970, the vehicles used in the marathon were often elderly, traditional wooden ones.

At a competition held at Windsor, a back wheel collapsed on a vehicle. The Queen was watching and saw this happen. A groom asked the Queen if they could cut down a small tree to tie to the back axle to keep it off the ground, to which she agreed. Miraculously the vehicle crossed the finish line on three wheels and a branch, much to everyone's amusement! That is why the rulebook now includes 'vehicle must have four wheels crossing the finishing line'. *(extracted from FEI website).*

Three-day competitions

These are at National level. Many club competitors feel it's just a step too far to be able to compete at them. Fear not, it *is* possible! The first step is qualifying at club level in the Novice Single Horse or Pony Class which will take you through to the National Championships held at Windsor in September each year. Although a three-day event, most people will arrive at Windsor on the Wednesday or Thursday, get parked up and settled and give their pony a day off after a possibly long journey.

For Intermediate, Open and Advanced National drivers there are events held throughout the summer where results count for qualification to the Championships. The procedure regarding your paperwork is similar to that already described for club events. You collect it from the stable manager and at this point you fill in a declaration form with details of your equine and pay a start fee. You must have your pony's passport to hand as well.

Familiarise yourself with where your dressage arena is situated and do walk it. Friday is dressage all day for all the classes. If you are in a Novice Class you may have a standing presentation around half an hour before your dressage time. Once you have completed your test and put your pony away, the day is yours to walk obstacles and sort out your vehicle for the marathon. One thing I find interesting is to watch other classes doing dressage. Not only can you watch the stars of the sport, but also learn how to drive other tests and present your pony to the best standards. Don't waste this opportunity.

On the Friday evening there will be a competitors' briefing, which you *must* attend with your backstepper – all information given will be useful. You will get the chance to meet some of the officials who put so much work into the sport. Marathon day will follow much the same procedure as a club day but you will see many more judges and officials. Please take time to have a chat and thank them. You will discover many are past competitors with stories to tell and really good tips to pass on.

As you arrive at the 10 minute halt your pony will be checked by a vet for heart and respiratory rates. Before you leave the rest area the vet will check the pony again and provided the rates have fallen to an acceptable level you will be allowed to the start of Section E. It is not often a pony is 'spun' out of the event at a halt but it can happen, especially in hot weather.

The obstacles at National three-day events are built with large sections of timber and seem huge in comparison to most club events. Their construction, design and dressing are to an exacting standard and make the occasion even more special. There will also be a commentator who will add excitement and give out interesting facts about the drivers and their horses. When you have completed your round and handed your section card in, a judge will be at the finish to check all was all right. If you have any doubts about anything – say so!

Sort out your pony and then go back to the obstacles to watch – it's great fun and adds to the enjoyment of your day. You will see how others tackle the routes and be amazed at the skill and speed of the team drivers. Keep an eye on the scoreboard for your class results and remember that any disputes must be brought to the scorer's attention within 30 minutes. Celebrations can go on for a lot longer! In the evening there is usually a beer tent and entertainment of some sort. The driving fraternity certainly do know how to enjoy themselves, so don't miss it!

The cones often start early – so a hangover is not to be recommended although having said that, many a competition has been won in a 'fragile' state. The cones are run in reverse order of placing so if you are in the lead in your class you will definitely be under pressure by the time you go in! The overall prizes for the class will be presented in the arena with your turnout. Prize winners do a lap of honour, and the winner does another on their own. You are then free to go home, once packing up and cleaning up is done. Before you leave, thank the stable manager for looking after you and when you get home write a letter of thanks to the organiser. The sport is small, no one is paid a salary for their time, so a little appreciation goes a long way to making the event happen again next year.

There is a basic checklist reminding you of some of the important things you need to remember at Appendix 5

Scoring

This is such a complicated subject to write about that I am only going to cover a very simplistic view of it. Tom Petitpierre who is the chief scorer for the BHDTA has the subject well sorted having done it for many years. He has shared this information and I really hope you will all have sympathies when things are incorrect: not frustrations.

Dressage – if you score an 8 for a movement it will become 2 penalties towards your final score; if you score 2 for a movement you will then get 8 penalties towards your final score. The fewer penalties the better the score. The FEI in their wisdom have decided to work on 160 points as a maximum therefore if your test has a total of 200 it is reduced to a maximum of 160 by multiplying by a factor of 0.8. This puts all tests on a level pegging.

Cones – the time is now down to 100ths of a second with 0.5 penalties being given for every second over the maximum time. 3 penalties are given for each ball down.

Marathon – for the obstacles the total time is added for all the obstacles then converted to penalties by dividing by 0.2. (0.2 penalties per second). The scoreboard shows the individual obstacle times in 100ths seconds and the total time taken. This time is then converted to penalties and added to any time penalties in the sections and put in the total column for the marathon. Section time penalties are 0.2 per second for exceeding the time allowed and 0.1 per second for being less than the time allowed.

As you can see this is an extremely complicated subject. As long as you have a basic knowledge of your penalties then leave the complexity to the specialists. Not being a 'figures' person my brain would be scrambled in the first five minutes! I am quite sure that they would be happy to give you an in depth explanation when they have time!

Stewards

The stewards hold the events together and make it possible for us to enjoy Driving Trials. Many are retired drivers who like to give something back to the sport, others just love the venues and horses, some are competitors who are addicted to their driving and like to share the workload.

Each steward will be given an area of responsibility for the day, whether it be time keeping, observing, writing for a judge, section steward or collecting ring, to name but a few. Even if you are uptight about something, please do not be rude or curt to these people because of your frustration if things aren't going to plan. It only takes one incident to put off stewards who come at their own expense to make it possible for you to enjoy yourself. Be courteous at all times. If you feel there are any discrepancies then go to the Judge or Technical Delegate who will have the responsibility to sort out such issues.

Young Drivers

No sport can have a future without youngsters participating. One of the main stumbling blocks with driving is the image of older people dominating and governing it. There is only grudging acceptance in some courts of young drivers taking the spoils. Thankfully this is being addressed across all driving disciplines and opportunities for young people are opening up. The BDS have Junior Scholarship awards; the BHDTA have the British Young Drivers section with training opportunities and competitions backed by the Training Committee and their passionate chairperson, Sydney Smith.

British Young Drivers' logo.

The rules have been changed to officially allow juniors from five to twenty-five years of age to be covered through the BHDTA and compete. Clubs are slowly being persuaded to allow this despite some resistance. The Scottish organisers of club events have been very accommodating enabling young drivers to get out and experience competition. This is really starting to pay off as fourteen to fifteen year olds are now very experienced and able to push drivers in Open Classes! If you hold back the enthusiastic child at six or seven and tell them they can't compete until they are fourteen, it's just too late. We coach children as young as four and let them compete at indoor competitions and they love it! The sense of responsibility and achievement spills over to other aspects of their lives.

There is now a National Championship for Young Drivers, which is another big step forward. This really gives them the feel of an adult national event and points them towards the goal of international competition.

Club Fun Days and Pleasure Drives

At Club Fun Days it is down to the organisers how they schedule the event, just phone beforehand and they will be happy to explain. At a Pleasure Drive you will be given a start time for the group to assemble. So make sure you allow enough time to find the venue, unload, harness up and put to. There is nothing worse than being late! These events are great for gaining experience without being put under the pressure of competition.

Talented young drivers from England, Ireland and Scotland competing at the National Junior Championships 2005.

Junior drivers performing their Musical Drive at the Opening Ceremony of the World Championships for Ponies at Catton Park in 2005.

9 The Fun Element

Finally, I think the most important point I would like to share is the fun element of driving. For pure pleasure you can't put a price on it – that amazing sense of achievement when you produce a pony to the level that you want. Not everyone wants to be a National level driver but that should not detract from the

Pure pleasure!

Father Christmas delivering his parcels!

enjoyment, or be scorned by those who do. I have competed successfully at National level and set my goals high because that was my ambition at that time. But I can honestly say that I am enjoying my new spotty ponies more than ever, even though I haven't yet targeted a goal for them, (doesn't mean I have lost my competitive edge, it's just biding its time!)

There are many avenues to explore for the fun side of driving as we said right at the beginning; the following are just a few.

BDS Trec

This is a new and very popular activity loosely based on the original French idea of Le Trec which is basically 'orienteering on horseback'! The BDS has drawn up a three-phase driven variety which requires you to find your way across country using map reading skills, keeping to a measured pace over the distance specified. It is usually quite a gentle one!

A typical route for BDS Trec.

A delightful picture at the start of a drive. The driver should have the whip in her hand though!

The first phase of the event is a safety presentation with points awarded or deducted for harnessing procedure and fitting; correct putting to; driver and groom's attire and suitability; essential spares kit and any other safety features like fluorescent tabards or carrying a mobile phone.

Then follows a drive-out into the country on quiet lanes or tracks; usually between 5 and 8 miles distance, turnouts leaving at intervals with maps, instructions and score cards. A couple of checkpoints are usually set up along the route at which a steward will mark the scorecard with time of arrival, within an allowance of 1 minute either way of the time specified. A compulsory walk section may be included with points deducted for break of pace. Your groom definitely needs to be able to map read!

Phase 3 of the event requires turnouts to attempt a minimum of six skills, with marks awarded for the skilful completion of each one. These can include reversing in a straight line, trotting a one-handed circle, negotiating a cones course, a motionless standstill, or any other ideas that the organiser may have that will demonstrate safe and skilled driving/backstepping.

An Hourglass formation that I put together for the Display. We were able to jump this turnout as the shape of the formation enabled each pony to see the jumps as he came up to them.

Events are held throughout the year organised around the country by local BDS centres culminating in a National Championship at the end of the season. This is a great way to get out with your pony and carriage, experience driving out in the country with the backup of knowledgeable and helpful people.

Cantering in the sea with my first stunt driving display pony, Mr Pie (my stunt career was all his fault – he got bored very easily and loved to play games and do tricks!).

Pleasure Driving

To my eyes this term encompasses most of the time on a carriage! The BDS has a good following through their area branches for various group or social activities. It's very relaxing meeting up with a group of like minded people, driving around a beautiful private estate or other area that might otherwise be unavailable to you. These drives are often followed by a barbeque or high tea – a super stress buster! There are also some longer endurance type drives organised around the country and you can find information on these through the driving press and websites.

Indoor Driving

Indoor carriage driving events usually held on one day have become increasingly popular, spearheaded by Dick Carey who set up the Indoor Carriage Driving Company in the late 1990s. Dick is forward thinking with innovative ideas and supported by a hardworking team. Regional competitions are held throughout the UK between October and March, culminating in a two-day final Championship just before the outdoor club season starts. If you are new to the sport I think this is the best place to start competing and I make it a goal for many of my clients, young and not so young drivers, when they first start. The environment is as safe as it is feasible to make it. Obviously the usual safety issues need addressing and the competitor must respect the fact that indoor surfaces make the carriage handle in a different way to grass. One blessing is that the dressage test is only about five minutes long and involves different criteria to outdoor tests – paces and precision being the benchmark. Many ponies that are brilliant schoolmasters are not the most supple or light on the bit. Outdoor dressage scoring would penalise them a lot, whereas indoor judging looks at rhythm, tempo and accuracy.

The cones phase is no more than ten cones which can include a serpentine. The optimum time is set at 220 metres per minute. Penalties are awarded for both over and under the time allowed, each second being one penalty point.

Lucy the Shetland pony at an indoor event with a young driver learning the skills of competition.

For the final phase two obstacles are built in the arena at either end with one start and finish gate serving both elements. The remit is to drive both obstacles in the correct order, starting only when indicated, and through the gates in the right direction! When all turnouts have completed these first two obstacles, the gates are re-lettered and drivers have a short time to re-walk them before driving again. The class winner will be the one with the least penalty points at the end of the day.

Some areas may vary slightly as to how they organise these competitions, but the format will be similar. I love them and thrive on having all the action on the one day. The Indoor Carriage Driving Club is the first club to have their own rules alongside of the BHDTA

*TOP: My backstepper working very hard to keep the balance as the pair fly round a turn. Exciting stuff!
ABOVE: Driver and groom well focussed on their next turn.*

Competing at an indoor event.

rules. Unlike outdoor competitions they allow a competitor to compete with two separate turnouts, in different classes, at an event. This is so refreshing and more in line with other equestrian disciplines where riders can compete a number of horses at the same event.

Drivers with Disabilities

Carriage driving is one of the few sports where drivers with disabilities can compete alongside able-bodied competitors. This is very much in demand and there are sufficient competitors worldwide to run a World Championship every two years. Britain is consistently in the medals at this and has a really good training structure with great opportunities available.

There are a hundred groups run alongside Riding for the Disabled Association with opportunities for over 1,000 drivers. The first group was formed in 1975 and each driver can progress through the range of proficiency tests to demonstrate their knowledge and ability. The groups used trained able-bodied volunteers known as AB whips, who sit alongside the driver and offer help and instruction. A number of disabled drivers are extremely capable and ambitious and we see many of them in competition alongside us at both indoor and BHDTA national events.

Top Tip:
At indoor competitions cones are scored as 5 penalties for each knockdown plus a penalty for each second off the optimum time. In the obstacles each knockdown is also 5 penalties and each commenced second in the obstacle is 1 penalty.

TOP: Heather Clarke who is consistently placed with her pony in competition against able-bodied rivals.
ABOVE: James Marshall, amazing with his horse pair. He is larger than life and always up to tricks on party night!

ABOVE:
Andy driving his
wheelchair adapted fun
bug at an indoor event. A
former sailor applying
excellent steering skills in
the cones.

ABOVE:
Andy driving his
wheelchair adapted fun
bug at an indoor event. A
former sailor applying
excellent steering skills in
the cones.

RIGHT:
Carolyn Fraser who is
partially sighted at her first
outdoor competition.
Anything is possible!

Driven Gymkhana

Driven gymkhana games are not extensively seen but are enormous fun and a different way to bring driving to the attention of people. The Sports Driving group offer this facility at their Try Driving Days and it is very popular with the Pony Club, Riding Clubs and Equestrian Centres. The rules are very simple: each team has an experienced driver on a Fun Bug (refer back to chapter 3 – this is the very safe carriage with no wheel spokes to cause injury). A team of four people take it in turns to perform the game and the first completed team over the line is the winner. This requires fit ponies and accurate driving in order to get close enough to poles and cones for the passenger to lean out and gather the items.

Concentration from all three! One team member putting a pole in the cone before crossing the start line and handing over to another member.

Final thoughts on Sports Driving

Sports Driving is an overall title to cover the various facets of competitive and pleasure driving. The idea being to bring together equestrian people to the joys of modern driving and to eliminate the stuffy attitude that carriage driving may have associated with it. Our aim is to make the sport available to those who may not ever have thought about trying it. There is no 'mystique' to driving; the pony is still the same functioning 'person' as a riding pony, and needs to be treated the same. The crossover in technique is so similar that it really does make the transition from saddle to box seat feasible.

A small group of dedicated drivers have formed the Sports Driving initiative which makes available to all the delights of driving. There are centres throughout the country where you can go to 'Try Driving' and learn the thrills and excitement. The Sports Driving group also have a travelling roadshow which can come to a centre near you and give a day long driving experience!

Driving is fun, fantastic and fulfilling! Brenda Hodgson, Gold and Bronze World Medallist with her stalwart pair of mother and daughter.

Appendix 1

Arenas

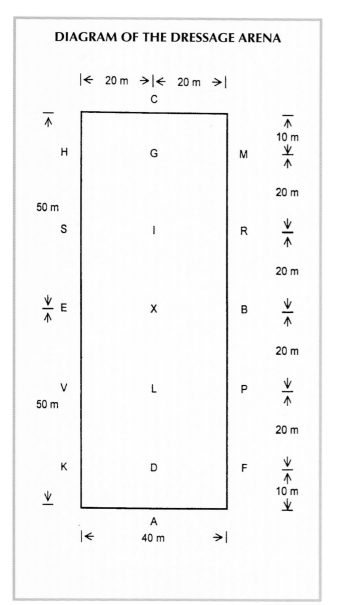

DIAGRAM OF THE DRESSAGE ARENA

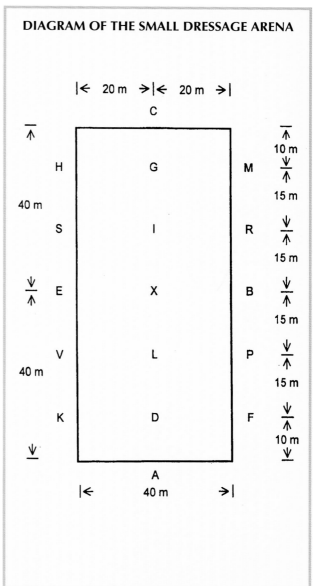

DIAGRAM OF THE SMALL DRESSAGE ARENA

Some Common Dressage Movements

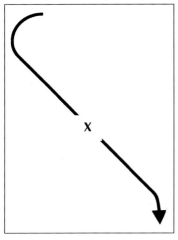

Diagonal

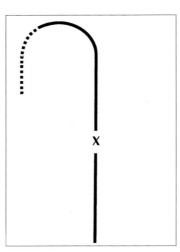

Turn off centre line

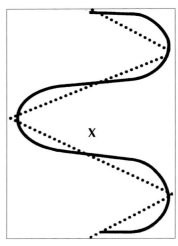

3 loop serpentine – dotted line
indicates incorrect route

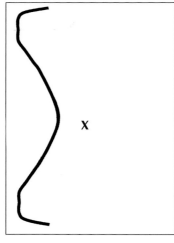

Deviation

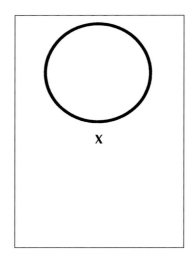

30 metre circle
in an 80×40 arena

Appendix 2

Marathon Speed/Distance Chart – Speed/Distance/Time

km	12kph		13kph		14kph		15kph		16kph		17kph		18kph		19kph		20kph		
KM	min	sec	min	sec	min	sec	min	sec	min	sec	min	sec	min	sec	min	sec	min	sec	KM
1	5	00	4	37	4	17	4	00	3	45	3	32	3	20	3	10	3	00	1
1.5	7	30	6	55	6	26	6	00	5	38	5	17	5	00	4	44	4	30	1.5
2	10	00	9	14	8	34	8	00	7	30	7	04	6	40	6	19	6	00	2
2.5	12	30	11	32	10	43	10	00	9	23	8	49	8	20	7	53	7	30	2.5
3	15	00	13	51	12	52	12	00	11	15	10	35	10	00	9	28	9	00	3
3.5	17	30	16	09	15	00	14	00	13	08	12	21	11	40	11	05	10	30	3.5
4	20	00	18	28	17	08	16	00	15	00	14	07	13	21	12	38	12	00	4
4.5	22	30	20	46	19	17	18	00	16	53	15	53	15	00	14	13	13	30	4.5
5	25	00	23	05	21	26	20	00	18	45	17	39	16	40	15	47	15	00	5
5.5	27	30	25	23	23	34	22	00	20	38	19	25	18	20	17	22	16	30	5.5
6	30	00	27	41	25	43	24	00	22	30	21	11	20	00	18	57	18	00	6
6.5	32	30	30	00	27	52	26	00	24	23	22	56	21	40	20	32	19	30	6.5
7	35	00	32	19	30	00	28	00	26	15	24	43	23	20	22	07	21	00	7
7.5	37	30	34	37	32	08	30	00	28	08	26	28	25	00	23	41	22	30	7.5
8	40	00	36	55	34	17	32	00	30	00	28	14	26	40	25	16	24	00	8
8.5	42	30	39	14	36	27	34	00	31	53	30	00	28	33	26	50	25	30	8.5
9	45	00	41	32	38	34	36	00	33	45	31	46	30	00	28	25	27	00	9
9.5	47	30	43	51	40	43	38	00	35	38	33	32	31	40	30	00	28	30	9.5
10	50	00	46	09	42	52	40	00	37	30	35	17	33	20	31	35	30	00	10
10.5	52	30	48	28	45	00	42	00	39	23	37	04	35	00	33	10	31	30	10.5
11	55	00	50	46	47	08	44	00	41	15	38	49	36	40	34	44	33	00	11
11.5	57	30	53	05	49	17	46	00	43	08	40	39	38	20	36	19	34	30	11.5
12	60	00	55	23	51	26	48	00	45	00	42	21	40	00	37	53	36	00	12
12.5	62	30	7	41	53	34	50	00	46	53	44	07	41	40	39	28	37	30	12.5
13	65	00	60	00	55	43	52	00	48	45	45	53	43	20	41	03	39	00	13
13.5	67	30	62	19	57	52	54	00	50	38	47	39	45	00	42	38	40	30	13.5
14	70	00	64	37	60	00	56	00	52	30	49	25	46	40	44	13	42	00	14
14.5	72	30	66	55	62	14	58	00	54	23	51	11	48	20	45	47	43	30	14.5
15	75	00	69	14	64	17	60	00	56	15	52	56	50	00	47	22	45	00	15
15.5	77	30	71	32	66	27	62	00	58	08	54	43	51	40	48	57	46	30	15.5
16	80	00	73	51	68	34	64	00	60	00	56	28	53	20	50	32	48	00	16
KM	12kph		13kph		14kph		15kph		16kph		17kph		18kph		19kph		20kph		KM

Appendix 3

Marathon Time Chart – 50m-1Km

M	12kph min	sec	13kph min	sec	14kph min	sec	15kph min	sec	16kph min	sec	17kph min	sec	18kph min	sec	19kph min	sec	20kph min	sec	M
50		15		14		13		12		11		11		10		10		09	50
100		30		28		26		24		23		21		21		19		18	100
200	1	00		55		52		48		45		43		40		38		38	200
300	1	30	1	38	1	17	1	12	1	08	1	04	1	00		57		54	300
400	2	00	1	51	1	43	1	36	1	30	1	25	1	21	1	16	1	12	400
500	2	30	2	19	2	08	2	00	1	88	1	46	1	40	1	35	1	30	500
600	3	00	2	46	2	34	2	24	2	15	2	07	2	00	1	53	1	48	600
700	3	30	3	14	3	00	2	48	2	38•	2	28	2	21	2	13	2	06	700
800	4	00	3	41	3	26	3	12	3	00	2	49	2	40	2	32	2	24	800
900	4	30	4	09	3	52	3	36	3	23	3	11	3	00	2	50	2	42	900
1K	5	00	4	37	4	17	4	00	3	45	3	32	3	21	3	10	3	00	1K
M	12kph		13kph		14kph		15kph		16kph		17kph		18kph		19kph		20kph		M

Appendix 4

Marathon Time Card

```
┌─────────────────────────────────────────────────┐
│                                                   │
│   The British Horse Driving Trials Association    │
│           MARATHON TIME CARD                      │
│                                                   │
│   COMPETITOR NO.  ...............................  │
│                                                   │
│                        TIME        Initials of    │
│                Hour   Min   Secs   Timekeeper     │
│   ┌──────────┬──────────────────┬──────────────┐ │
│   │ START A  │   :       :       │              │ │
│   ├──────────┼──────────────────┼──────────────┤ │
│   │ FINISH A │   :       :       │              │ │
│   ├──────────┼──────────────────┼──────────────┤ │
│   │ START B  │   :       :       │              │ │
│   ├──────────┼──────────────────┼──────────────┤ │
│   │ FINISH B │   :       :       │              │ │
│   ├──────────┼──────────────────┼──────────────┤ │
│   │ START C  │   :       :       │              │ │
│   ├──────────┼──────────────────┼──────────────┤ │
│   │ FINISH C │   :       :       │              │ │
│   ├──────────┼──────────────────┼──────────────┤ │
│   │ START D  │   :       :       │              │ │
│   ├──────────┼──────────────────┼──────────────┤ │
│   │ FINISH D │   :       :       │              │ │
│   ├──────────┼──────────────────┼──────────────┤ │
│   │ START E  │   :       :       │              │ │
│   ├──────────┼──────────────────┼──────────────┤ │
│   │ FINISH E │   :       :       │              │ │
│   └──────────┴──────────────────┴──────────────┘ │
└─────────────────────────────────────────────────┘
```

Appendix 5

Competition Quick Reference Checklist

Dressage

- Wear allocated number
- Spares
- Hat compulsory for everyone
- Apron required for driver and brown gloves for both driver and groom
- Groom must remain seated
- Groom must not talk
- Whip must be carried at all times
- Groom must not dismount or touch reins in the arena, except for safety reasons
- No boots on horse – (although some clubs may allow this)
- Lamps required at National level
- Correct wheel width – same as cones
- Smile!

Cones

- Walk course (without your groom)
- Wear allocated number
- Spares
- Hat compulsory for everyone
- Groom must remain seated
- Groom must not talk – driver not to speak to groom
- Whip must be carried at all times
- Groom must not dismount or touch reins, except for safety reasons
- Correct wheel width required
- Crossing your tracks is permitted
- Must not start the course until whistle/bell or other indication
- Lamps optional at National level but must have reflectors fitted
- Same vehicle must be used for both dressage and cones

Marathon

- Walk obstacles
- Be at the start 10 minutes early
- Wear allocated number in a bib
- Crash hats must be worn and fastened at all times
- Remember stop watches
- Remember timesheet
- Spares
- Groom must not dismount during competition except for emergency or at halts
- Watch for compulsory flags/km markers
- Section A – any pace
- Section B – walk – 5 second break of pace allowed
- Section C – fast trot – 5 second break of pace allowed } Before being penalised
- Section D – walk – 5 second break of pace allowed
- Section E – trot or walk except in obstacles, must return to trot within 5 seconds of obstacle exit gates
- 10 penalties for groom dismounting within obstacle
- Groom must not touch whip or reins
- Talking is permissible (no arguments please!)
- Hold up procedure: During the marathon it may be necessary to stop competitors on the course for various reasons. The stewards will ask you to halt and wait until the obstruction is cleared, then re-start you. They will tell you for how many minutes you have been held up and it is imperative that you make a note of this in order to adjust your time sheet accordingly. I do suggest if this happens you stop one of the watches and then re-start it when the steward sets you off again. This will keep you to your original timings without having to deduct the hold up period every time you synchronise with your time sheet.

Appendix 6 – Suggested layout for marathon time sheet

Section A									Section B	Section C				Section D	Section E								
1	2	3	4	5	6	7	8	9		1	2	3	4		1	2	3	4	5	6	7	8	9
Min Max										Min Max					Min Max								

Appendix 7

References and Bibliography – Useful organisations:

British Driving Society
BDS Executive Secretary
83 New Road
Helmingham
Stowmarket
Suffolk
IP14 6EA
Tel: 01473 892001
Fax: 01473 892005
email@britishdrivingsociety.co.uk
www.britishdrivingsociety.co.uk

British Horse Driving Trials Association
Stoneleigh Park
Kenilworth
Warwickshire
CV8 2LG
Tel. 02476 419 078
Fax : 02476 419 079
bhdta@horsedrivingtrials.co.uk
www.horsedrivingtrials.co.uk

British Horse Society
Stoneleigh Deer Park
Kenilworth,
Warwickshire
CV8 2XZ
Tel: 08701 202244
Fax :01926 707800
enquiry@bhs.org.uk
www.bhs.org.uk

Sports Driving
Sue Mart
4 Sparrow Lane
Long Bennington
Newark
Notts
NG23 5DL
01400 281280
artisticiron@btconnect.com
www.sportsdriving.co.uk

Riding for the Disabled Association
Lavinia Norfolk House,
Avenue R,
Stoneleigh Park,
Warwickshire
CV8 2LY
Tel: 0845 658 1082
Fax: 0845 658 1083
www.riding-for-disabled.org.uk

Scottish Carriage Driving Association
SCDA Secretary
East Overhill
Stewarton
Ayrshire
KA3 5JT
Telephone: 0845 226 9498
secretary@scda.co.uk
www.scda.co.uk

Indoor Carriage Driving Company
Parish Farm
Mill Lane
Hooe
Nr Battle
East Sussex
TN33 9HS
dickcarey@indoorcarriage.orangehome.co.uk
www.indoordriving.co.uk

Useful websites:

Carriage Driving Global	www.carriage-driving.com	Useful reference site with many links
Carriage Link	www.carriagelink.com	Site selling anything to do with driving
Carriage Driving Info	www.carriagedriving.info	Directory of carriage driving sites on the net
Carriage Sales	www.carriagesales.com	Site selling carriages
Carriage Horse	www.carriagehorse.co.uk/	Carriage horse enthusiast's website
FEI	www.horsesport.org	Governing body of equestrian sport
Scurry Driving Association	www.scurrydrivers.co.uk	Governing body of Scurry Driving
Carriage Driving Ireland	www.carriagedrivingireland.com	Irish Carriage Driving organisation
Driving Horse	www.drivinghorse.co.uk	On-line marketplace for all things driving
Native Pony	www.thenativepony.com	Site for native pony enthusiasts
Harness Horse	www.harnesshorse.co.uk	On-line marketplace for all things driving
Shetland Pony Society	www.shetlandponystudbooksociety.co.uk	Shetland Pony Breed Society
Dartmoor Hill Pony	www.dartmoorhillpony.com	Dartmoor Pony Breed Society
British Spotted Pony Society	www.britishspottedpony.com	British Spotted Pony Breed Society
Spotted Horse and Pony Society	www.thespottedhorseandponysociety.com	Spotted Horse and Pony Society
Welsh Pony and Cob Society	www.wpcs.uk.com	Welsh Pony and Cob Society
Welsh Cob Society	www.welshcob.co.uk	Welsh Cob Breed Society

Appendix 8

Bibliography

The following is a list of carriage driving books, which will make useful additions to your library either to dip into, or for referece.

Carriage Driving, John Cowdery, Crowood Press

The Encyclopaedia of Carriage Driving, Sallie Walrond, J A Allen

Make the Most of Carriage Driving, Vivian & Richard Elllis and Joy Claxton, J A Allen

The Principles of Carriage Driving, German National Equestrian Federation, Kenilworth Press

Competition Carriage Driving, HRH The Duke of Edinburgh, J A Allen

Driving and Judging Dressage, HRH The Duke of Edinburgh, J A Allen

Looking at Carriages, Sallie Walrond, J A Allen

30 years on and off The Box Seat, HRH The Duke of Edinburgh, J A Allen

The Art of Driving, Max Pape, J A Allen

The Allen Illustrated Guide to Bits and Bitting, Hilary Vernon, J A Allen

Hints on Driving, Captain G Morley Knight, J A Allen

Schooling Horses in Hand, Richard Hinrichs, J A Allen

Index

(*numbers in italics refer to illustrations*)

The smiles say it all